How to Start a Blog

MAKE MONEY ONLINE IN 2020. A STEP BY STEP GUIDE TO PROMOTE YOUR BUSINESS

SARAH MILLER − VANESSA MANSON

© **Copyright 2019 - All rights reserved.**

The content contained within this book may not be reproduced, duplicated or transmitted without direct written permission from the author or the publisher.

Under no circumstances will any blame or legal responsibility be held against the publisher, or author, for any damages, reparation, or monetary loss due to the information contained within this book, either directly or indirectly.

Legal Notice:

This book is copyright protected. It is only for personal use. You cannot amend, distribute, sell, use, quote or paraphrase any part, or the content within this book, without the consent of the author or publisher.

Disclaimer Notice:

Please note the information contained within this document is for educational and entertainment purposes only. All effort has been executed to present accurate, up to date, reliable, complete information. No warranties of any kind are declared or implied. Readers acknowledge that the author is not engaging in the rendering of legal, financial, medical or professional advice. The content within this book has been derived from various sources. Please consult a licensed professional before attempting any techniques outlined in this book.

By reading this document, the reader agrees that under no circumstances is the author responsible for any losses, direct or indirect, that are incurred as a result of the use of the information contained within this document, including, but not limited to, errors, omissions, or inaccuracies.

TABLE OF CONTENTS

Introduction

Chapter 1: An Introduction to Blogging

What Is a Blog?

What Makes a Blog Identifiable?

Should You Start a Blog?

Chapter 2: The Framework of Your Blog

Selecting a Topic for Your Blog

Defining Your Goals

Tips for a Successful Blog

Thinking about the Future

Ethics When Blogging

How to Remain Truthful

Keeping Your Reputation and Privacy Protected

Chapter 3: Creating Your Blog

Creating a Blogger Blog

Using WordPress

Microblogging with Tumblr

How to Customize Your Blog

How to Name Your Blog

Chapter 4: Blogging with More than Words

Why Should You Use Images in Your Blog?

What Is Podcasting?

Wrap Up

Chapter 5: Promoting Your Blog

Networking

Guest Posting

Posting Useful Comments on Other Blogs

Improving Search Result Rankings and SEO

Include Social Media Sharing Buttons on Your Blog

Repurpose Content

Visit Up-Vote Communities and Aggregate Sites

Promoting Your Blog on Social Media Networks

Don't Ignore Social Bookmarking Sites

Search for Forums and Join the Discussion

Go for Paid Promotion

Chapter 6: Making Money Blogging

Affiliate Marketing

Creating a Membership Site

Selling Digital Products on Your Blog

Sell Physical Products

Offer Paid Consultation

Pay-Per-Click Advertising (PPC)

Sell Your Blog Space to Private Advertisers

Sponsored Posts

Blog Flipping

Chapter 7: Promoting Your Blog and Making Money through Email Marketing

What Is Email Marketing?

Benefits of Email Marketing

Building an Email List

Email List Segmentation

Tracking through Google Analytics

What Can You Sell through an Email Marketing Campaign?

Chapter 8: How to Form a Blog Monetization Strategy

Identifying What the Market Wants

Expanding Your Sources of Incoming Traffic

Developing the Hub of the Business

Leads Acquisition

Sales Generation

Growing Your Community

How Much Can You Make Blogging?

Conclusion

References

Introduction

Working long hours can take its toll on you both physically and mentally. The daily commute, the lack of passion, and the unethical people-pleasing habits that you develop are just some of the issues. Without proper self-care, you may also develop stress in the process.

Knowing this, you need a solution to earn more income while cutting down on the time you spend working a regular job and you have decided to go into the blogosphere. The only issue is that you do not know how to create a successful blog or make money from the blog.

This is a problem that a lot of people face when they decide to start blogging. It is also the reason why people quit a few years into blogging. In this book, I will empower you with vital information that can change your life for good.

The methods I introduce in this book have been tested and mentioned by some of the most successful blogs on the internet. This information can help you overcome the various issues that people face during the initial stages of blogging.

My experience in the blogosphere spans over ten years. During the period I started blogging, it was merely a means to overcome my boredom. I was also fascinated by the possibility of interacting with other internet users by sharing the knowledge I have acquired over the years.

From sharing life experiences to blogging about some of the topics that fascinated me, blogging gave me a way to reach out to my readers in ways that other social networks couldn't offer. It wasn't until a few years later that I came across the real goldmine in blogging.

Learning about the possibility of making money from blogging threw me off balance, so I could make something that excited me this much? For a few months after, I wasn't posting as much. I was developing a new strategy.

My new strategy involved making money from my blog. I was neck-deep in research learning the best ways to make money through my blog. This was my new motivation for blogging.

Forget the fancy stories you hear from some of the most popular bloggers. I won't tell you that it was easy making money from my blog during the initial period. There was a need for me to completely change every aspect of my blog to start bringing in money. There are not many advertisers that will take you seriously if your blog doesn't focus on a niche. The same applies when you are trying to sell an e-book or an online course to your readers. This is something I learned early.

These are some of the things I will teach you in this book. You can expect to find information on the various methods through which your blog can earn you money along with the right ways to promote your blog. This book is suitable for the development from an amateur to a professional blogger.

Some of the information you will find in this book include the following:

- The purpose of a blog
- Choosing a topic or niche for your blog
- Tips for growing your blog
- The need for thinking long-term when blogging
- Rules or ethics when blogging
- Promoting your blog
- Going beyond the use of plain texts in your blog

- How much you can make blogging

This and much more will be discussed in the various chapters of this book. In the end, you should have a better grip on how to make money blogging ethically.

I have had the opportunity to work as a consultant for some small businesses in creating their blogs. Also, I have practiced the option of blog flipping.

The skills I have gained from these experiences are immeasurable. These gave me the best opportunities to practice everything I learned from my research.

I still take time to visit the blogs of some of my past clients, and I'm happy to see that there is still a high level of engagement on these blogs. Everything I put into practice on these occasions is all contained herein.

I promise that if you take the time to apply the various strategies and tips I've introduced in this book, you will go on to build a profitable blog.

This book is a way for me to help you hone your blogging skills and help you to see the opportunities where they are quietly sitting.

If you have the opportunity to interact with some of the most popular bloggers, you will often hear them say that making money from blogging takes time. This is a fact, but you don't have to spend as much time as the others. For this reason, I urge you to start now.

The longer the start, the more time you have to wait before you start making money from your blog. You can change your situation today by taking action. Good things unquestionably happen to those who wait, but you can get better results if you make changes while you wait.

Everything you will find in this book is specially written to meet all your needs as a blogger. The book is designed to generate results if applied in the right way. Each chapter has information regarding different areas of blogging.

You must act on the information you learn from each chapter as soon as you complete it. Waiting till you finish the book isn't always the best option.

Once you start applying the tips in the book and seeing results, you will begin to look at your blog as more of a business and be more motivated in seeing it grow.

Chapter 1: An Introduction to Blogging

What Is a Blog?

In plain language, a blog is a type of website. What makes it unique is how you use it. Using or running a blog involves focusing on publishing written content that you refer to as a blog post or entry. There is no specific topic a blog must cover, which makes it easy to start one.

Blogs can focus on writing content using facts for informational purposes or posting fictional stories for purely entertainment purposes.

Blogs allow the blogger to connect directly with the audience through the comments sections.

This connection is what most bloggers crave and the reason why they come up with excellent content to update.

A blog can allow you to develop trust and loyalty with your readers, making it easier to share ideas. It is through this trust and loyalty that you can make money from a blog.

The value you can offer your audience makes them willing to pay for what you have to offer. This is a form of support they show to your blog.

What Makes a Blog Identifiable?

When you consider the types of content on the internet, it is okay if you find it difficult to differentiate a blog from a regular website.

Nonetheless, there are a few distinct features of a blog that you can use in identifying them. Here is a look at some of these features.

Creation of Posts

Every update on a blog is identifiable as a blog entry or a blog post. The owner of the blog creates this entry or post and then uploads it on the blog site.

A Reverse Chronological Order

The reverse chronological order refers to the way all the posts on a blog appear. In this order, the older posts appear lower on the page while newer posts appear at the top of the page.

If the blogger decides to upload a post any time, it will become the first post on the list of entries on the blog.

Categories

To simplify the process of searching for a post, a blog owner can decide to group the posts on a blog based on the topic it discusses. This is helpful to both the blog owner and the readers.

Social Sharing Buttons

The social sharing buttons you can find on a blog provides the opportunity for readers to share a post on various social media networks. There are other buttons that also allow readers to connect directly with the blogger on their social media channels.

These buttons can assist in promoting their blog and growing their followers on social media.

Comments Section

While it is a crucial part of the blog, not all blogs give room for readers to post comments. Nonetheless, on most of the identifiable blogs, there is a comments section that allows users to leave their responses and get a reply from the blogger.

Regular Updates

To maintain consistent incoming traffic, bloggers have to keep uploading entries or posts to their blogs. These are essential updates that offer fresh content to their readers. It can be on a daily or weekly basis.

You can find some blogs that receive these updates multiple times a day.

These blogs usually don't have a schedule for uploading posts, while others may follow a strict schedule. The schedule is to improve the chances of readers to see the latest post on the blog.

Permalinks

Permalink is a short form for "permanent link." It is a page that the blog software creates to display the latest post on the blog, along with the comments on this post. The process is repeated for every new update on the blog.

The benefit of this permalink is that it enhances your visibility on search engine results.

Archives

A blog will usually have an archive when the posts start piling up. This is a method through which the blog owner can sort the posts. It also makes it easy for readers to find older posts without scrolling too far.

The archive can sort posts according to date, or a blogger may decide to go for the theme-based approach in sorting their blog.

Search Function

Another excellent function that you can find on a blog is the search function.

This is a valuable tool that makes it possible for readers to find older posts without having to go through too much stress.

Type in the title of the post or a keyword to generate similar results on the blog.

Should You Start a Blog?

In all honesty, blogging isn't the right path for everyone. It requires a lot of time investment, dedication, and patience to create a blog that will attract a broad audience. If you lack patience, time, or dedication, then you shouldn't bother about blogging.

If you are ready to develop yourself in these areas, then you can look at some of the reasons why you should start a blog.

I believe that every one that is reading this book has these three qualities in their arsenal. They are the qualities that guide a successful blogger.

There are various reasons why you should start a blog. In answering this question, I will create two different subheadings.

The first is the purpose of a blog, and the second includes general reasons why you should start a blog.

The Purpose of a Blog

The purpose of a blog can vary depending on how you decide to use it. Different blogs have different purposes. This is often the outcome of what the blog owner decides to focus on when building the blog.

As an individual deciding to blog, your blog might have multiple purposes. Regardless, here is a look at the various goals you can have for your blog.

To Document Your Life Experiences

If you want a way to keep track of the various events that go on in your life, then a blog can be the answer. It can function in the same way as a diary.

It is also an excellent means through which you can post updates to friends and family about these events in your life.

To use your blog in this manner, you must be very comfortable sharing details of your personal life with random individuals.

You can go from sharing your vacation to discussing some of the most challenging times of your life.

While you may genuinely open the blog to keep your loved ones in the loop, remember that a blog is a public page that anyone can access.

For this reason, you have to think long-term when posting on a personal blog. Information that you believe will affect you negatively or embarrass you later should not appear on the blog.

To Share Information

Everyone is looking for information in one form or the other. The internet has become the best place to find this information.

The information you can find on the internet include news, DIY projects, life improvement tips, and many more.

You can open a blog to create a place where people can find the information they are looking for. It can be their source of daily inspiration or where they can get an update on the various events happening around them.

There is a wide range of topics that you can cover with an informational blog.

A commentator or critic can use an informational blog to share their predictions and opinions on certain events. If you know of the GSMArena blog, then you will have an idea of how they cover everything in technology.

These include phones, laptops, operating systems, software, cameras, and so much more. It is a valuable resource where you can get information on most of the latest updates in communications technology.

For Monetization

This is why you're currently reading this book — to make money through your blog. You are not the first to use a blog for this purpose and definitely won't be the last.

The opportunity to make money through a blog is endless. Although it requires a lot of time investment, it is a profitable venture that is impossible to overlook.

A blog is a platform that helps you develop influence over your readers or audience.

Monetizing your blog is merely putting this influence into use. You don't have to do anything unethical, like manipulating your readers into buying a substandard product.

You can place adverts, promote products, or sell your unique products. Using your writing skills, you can earn a decent amount from commissions when you join an affiliate program.

Companies are also taking advantage of the influence a blog can have over their target audience.

Numerous companies pay bloggers to mention their products, while others go as far as creating a blog for the business.

They then look to hire bloggers for freelance writing projects to build the blog.

Building a Community

If your daily life involves going to work in the morning and heading straight home later in the day, then you will have little time to interact with people outside work.

Some individuals who experience this may decide to use their blog to create a community where they can interact with other users at any time of the day.

It provides the opportunity to connect with individuals that share a like mind with you to discuss on an intellectual level.

If you develop your relationships right, a blog can be an excellent place to create new friends that you can meet in real life. Remember, there is always a need for balance. Don't let online communities replace the need for real-life interactions.

Blogging for a Cause

Some people have a much different motivation when creating a blog. This motivation may be the drive to make a difference in the world. That is what it means when you decide to promote a cause through a blog.

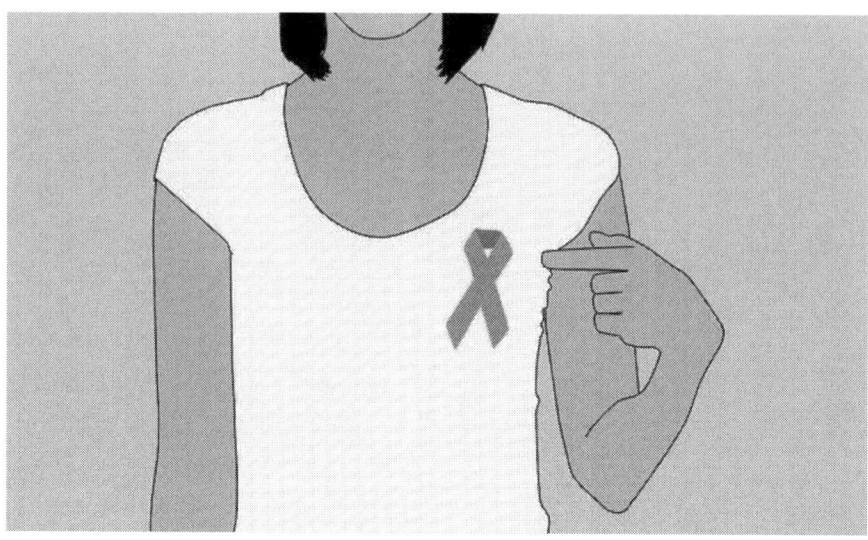

The purpose of the blog may be to raise awareness over a specific societal issue, such as drug abuse, while it will also offer support for victims in the process.

Such a blog can keep growing and go on to make a significant impact on a community or the world at large.

To Engage in Your Passion

The final purpose (and also one of the most common) I will introduce is the need to explore something you love doing. This is the reason why there are so many blogs on the internet today. It allows people to engage in their hobbies and passion.

With a blog, you can talk about these passions or hobbies as much as you want. Tell people about your personal experiences and let them learn from it. Seeing positive outcomes from those who learn from your experiences usually makes it worthwhile.

General Reasons Why You Should Start a Blog

For Self-Improvement

This is usually not the main reason for blogging, but this is one of the side effects of blogging. Through blogging, you can develop yourself as an individual. It also helps to create new opportunities for you.

In creating a successful blog, you have to improve both your communication and writing skills continually.

These are skills that you will retain for the rest of your life.

It addition, it is common for a blog to make you an asset to any employer. If you run a personal blog where you exhibit transparency, you can get a slight advantage.

Growing a Business

If you run a small business, then running a blog can be an excellent way to connect with potential customers. These customers want to work with a company that they are sure can meet their needs. This is what you can do with a blog.

You can establish yourself as an authority in your niche. Besides, you can also promote your products and services on the blog.

This makes it possible to reach customers who would otherwise be impossible with traditional marketing methods.

Assume the blog to be a promotional tool that you can use in showcasing yourself and your business to the world.

To Offer Assistance to Others

With both personal and informational blogs, there is the possibility of assisting someone going through a challenge.

Depending on the type of information you provide on your blog, you can help a person to get out of debt or make some changes to their lifestyle.

A personal blog provides a way for people to tap into one crucial resource — experience. Everyone will be willing to take a particular action if they know someone who has taken similar action with positive results.

They want to know what they are getting into and what to expect.

It Is Easy

I know this may come as a surprise to you, but blogging is easy. With lots of excellent tools like WordPress, you can develop a blog that outperforms some of the most expensive websites in design.

This is due to the possibility of customizing the themes and gaining access to several plugins to boost your blog.

Also, uploading a post on the blog is very easy.

Chapter 2: The Framework of Your Blog

Selecting a Topic for Your Blog

In the world of blogging, if there is one thing that will never be exhausted, it is blog topics. There will always be a topic to blog about regardless of what niche your blog is in.

With blogging, there are no limitations to how far you can go with a project or an idea.

While blogging seems to be ideally suited for ideas, projects, and hobbies, there is a lot more you can do with your blog. There are lots of blogs in existence, and these blogs were created for various purposes.

What I am trying to say is that you should not limit yourself to certain types of topics when blogging. As long as you have a blog, you can talk about anything.

Virtually everyone loves freedom. However, one thing that a lot of people fail to realize is that having enormous freedom comes with some challenges.

One of these challenges is having to deal with excess ideas since there are no limitations. While there is a high chance of this occurring to anyone who decides to blog, as a new blogger, you are free to blog about any topic of your choice and move in a definite direction once you find a niche that you are most comfortable in.

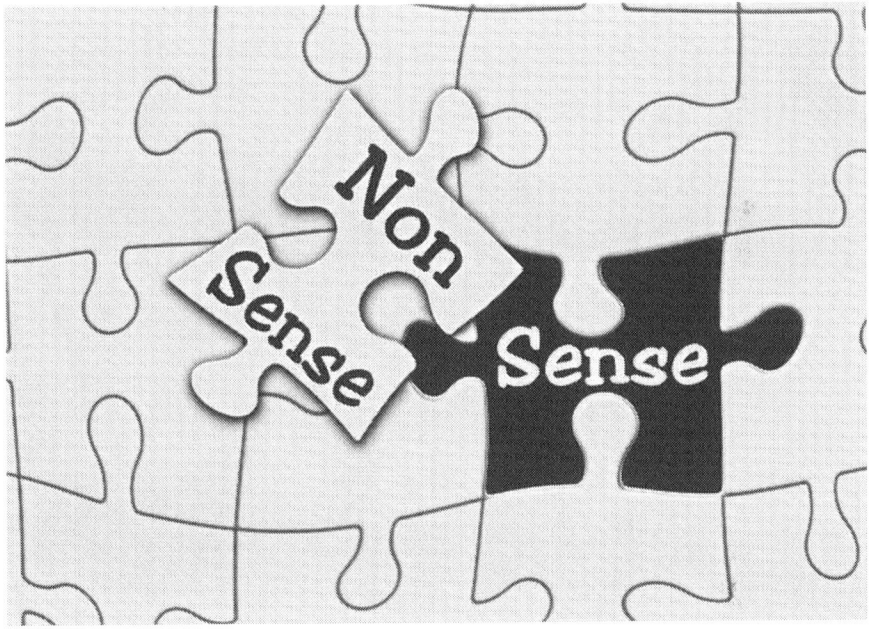

Although you might never be able to keep a post out of people's views because of the existence of screenshots, you do not have to leave a post on your blog if it is not in the direction you are going. You can always delete posts.

When starting a blog, some tips can help you to move in a definite direction faster. Below are some of them.

Focus on Genuine Interests

When starting a blog, a lot of people make the mistake of selecting a topic because they believe many are interested in it or because they think that blogging about a specific topic is more socially acceptable.

This is a wrong move because if you must keep writing in a particular direction, the easiest way to do this is to blog about something that you are genuinely interested in.

People are not just interested in reading the topics they love. They are interested in passionately written content.

Know What Topics Are Off-Limits

Although there is a lot of freedom with what one can blog about, as a blogger, there are certain topics that should be considered off-limits.

While this might contradict the idea of being limitless with the topic you decide to blog about, you might want to leave your personal life out of your blog.

Keep Your Readers in Mind

Every blog should have a target audience. When starting a blog, you should always have your prospective readers in mind. Think of who they are and what ways you can keep them interested in your blog.

Think about the number of readers you have on your blog and what you want them to know.

Defining Your Goals

There are lots of reasons why people blog. In the same vein, there are several ways to be successful as a blogger. When blogging, always bear in mind that your plans as a blogger might differ from those of other bloggers.

So as you go on with your blog, it is expedient that you always pay attention to your goals.

When looking to characterize a successful blog, you can make use of the ways below:

Fun

If fun is your principal reason for creating a blog, from time to time, it will be wise to carry out assessments to help you find out if you still get the right level of fun from your blog.

Comments

Lots of bloggers derive an excellent level of satisfaction from the interactions that they have with their readers. Bloggers with such interest will always feel successful if they have a good number of people commenting on every post they put up.

Results

Some bloggers set up blogs just because they need to carry out specific tasks. Some of these tasks include selling products and raising funds for charity. For bloggers in this category, achieving the goals for setting up their blog is synonymous to success.

Income

Certain people are motivated by money. Bloggers who fall into this category of people are a lot interested in converting a hobby into a source of income. Being able to do this will mean they are successful.

Numbers

It is the goal of most bloggers to have people flooding their blog daily. A lot of bloggers attribute success to the number of people who visit a blog every day.

It is vital that you set aside time to give thoughts to your definition of success.

✔ Are you interested in making people aware of the experiences you had on a journey?

✔ Are you writing a book and trying to make it popular?

To always keep your goals in mind, you should make them a part of your initial blog post. After blogging for a while, take some time to go through the posts containing your goals.

This will help you always stay on track.

Tips for a Successful Blog

Be Consistent

It is not enough to put up amazing posts on your blog. If you must make anything from blogging, you have to post regularly. Although the word "regularly" is quite straightforward, when it comes to posting on a blog, it might be interpreted by various people differently.

While different people might have different interpretations of "regularly," to get the best out of your blog and still have enough time for other things, you can limit your posts to three times every week.

This way, you will always be able to have the right amount of fresh posts on your blog and still have time for other activities.

The fact that you put up posts about three times a week does not imply that you should only write for your blog three times a week.

As a blogger, there are times you might experience writer's block. Also, you might want to go on vacation.

So to ensure that holidays or writer's block doesn't interfere with your posts, you can write posts and schedule them to be displayed at a particular time.

This way, you can always have something for your expectant readers even when you are physically not available to write.

Interact with Your Audience

Blogs differ from websites in various ways. One of these ways is the possibility of commenting on a post on blogs and building a relationship with the blog owner, as well as other readers of the blog.

While people can have conversations on forums, these conversations don't have the direction that blogs provide.

With blogs, visitors can always comment on a post just after going through it.

There are various reasons why readers comment on a post. Sometimes they put up comments because they want to make suggestions or ask questions.

Other times, they comment because it is the easiest way they can react to what they read.

Usually, blog posts come with links that are positioned just under a post. This link is typically an indication of the number of comments that such post has attracted.

When this link is clicked, it moves you to the page where the post is located. Also, it reveals the comments of other readers and an invite to comment.

When a reader comments on a blog post, this comment can be found in the section of a blog that is dedicated to comments. Such comments include the name of whoever made it. It also consists of the date, as well as the time of the comment.

While allowing comments is an excellent way to interact with readers, some blogs do not make provisions for people to make comments.

Famous bloggers usually own these types of blogs, and the reason this happens is that more often than not, famous bloggers get more comments than they can handle on their blog posts. So to ensure that they do not get overwhelmed by the number of comments after each post, they turn off the comments section after putting up a post.

While keeping up with the number of comments associated with a blog can be a challenge, this can be said to be a good challenge and one that a lot of bloggers look forward to encountering.

So before you get to the point where it is impossible to keep up with the comments on your blog, always ensure that the comments section of your blog is kept on. With the comments section of your blog enabled, your audience can still keep in touch with you.

Also, you can have first-hand information about what they think about your posts. While various blog platforms function differently, a lot of them give bloggers the freedom of allowing comments on individual posts and restricting them on others without ultimately affecting the settings of a blog.

This way, if you do not want any comments on a particular post, you can put the needed restrictions.

While comments make it very easy for bloggers to build a relationship with their readers, they come with a downside.

The downside is that spammers can use them. When your blog has its comments turned on, a lot of people will take advantage of this to put up unsolicited ad placements.

Thinking about the Future

It is quite reasonable for people to think short-term when they first get started with a project, and bloggers are not an exception. When a lot of people start blogs, they never really think about what they want the blog to be like in five years.

A lot of bloggers consider online years to have some things in common with dog years. Some of the most established bloggers have not been around for too long.

This is because of the drastic changes that characterize blogging. When starting a blog, you need to make up your mind on how long you intend to be blogging.

Will you be doing it for just a short while, or is it something you plan to do for a long time?

While it might not be straightforward to decide how long you want to blog and what you want your blog to be like in the near future, being able to provide answers to specific questions can be helpful.

Your Level of Commitment

Before providing an answer to this question, take out time to think of how committed you are to your blog.

How much priority do you give to your blog? If your blog is not one of those things you prioritize a lot, then there is a considerable likelihood that you might not remain a blogger for long.

However, if you are interested in making your business more visible with the use of your blog or keep your friends updated with the recent happenings in your life, blogging might be something you are cut out for.

While there are lots of ways to be sure of how committed you are to your blog, one trusted way to be sure of your level of commitment so far blogging is concerned is to decide on the number of posts you want to put up weekly or daily.

Lots of famous bloggers have a reputation for putting up posts daily. One reason for this is that their blogs are a source of income. Unlike blogs that already make some money for their owners, lots of personal blogs only get updated weekly.

Do You Derive Joy from Writing?

A lot of people can write. There is, however, a difference between having the ability to write and being able to create interesting and captivating content.

Blogging is not something to be learned rapidly. It is something that people get better at by doing it over a long period. If you are looking to make something out of blogging, to make this a reality, you will need a free test.

Simply head to www.blogger.com and create a free blog that will serve as your practice arena.

Once you have this blog created, try to put up posts consistently for a specified period. This way, you can detect if writing is something you can do on a long-term basis.

Before being sure of your writing abilities and how interested you are in blogging, you should not invest a lot of money and time into a blog.

While typing is a skill that is needed to blog, some people are not good at typing or even writing. If you have difficulties in writing or typing, you can try vlogging.

Will Your Blog Be Professional or Personal?

If a blog to you is something that should contain personal information, you might want to spend less time on your blog than you do on a job that pays you.

Also, you should operate on a lean budget if you are running a personal blog.

On the other hand, if you intend to operate a professional blog, your approach should be very different.

A professional blog should be treated like a business. Your design should be professional, and everything you do about your blog should be considered a business.

This implies that you should not blog when you are busy. You should have ample time in the day allocated for blogging.

Do You See Blogging as a New Career That Will Help You Meet More People Who Matter in the Society?

Websites are not just a place to put up information. Sometimes, they function as social networks. They help you connect with people.

Since blogs are used to reach out to people, if the people whom you are interested in reaching out to are made up of professionals, your blog can convey specific details that you are not interested in passing.

While you must pass the right message, this does not mean you should get all corporate.

It is possible to get into a new career path by merely owning a blog. This has happened several times in the past. This, however, is only possible when the blog is of high quality.

A lot of people have started TV shows and had great book deals just because they had successful blogs.

When starting a blog, there are lots of things you should think about. One of these things is what the needs of your audience are.

Also, the software you make use of when blogging is important. If you have intentions of making a lot from blogging, you will need to work with software that will make that a reality.

How Easy Is It for You to Share Details about Your Business or Personal Life?

The internet never forgets. Also, when you put up something on the internet, the people you are trying to reach are not the only ones who see it. People you had no plans reaching and you never knew existed can come across your posts.

After blogging for a while, bloggers soon realize that they are attracting more attention than they initially planned to attract.

Ethics When Blogging

It is good to be on the defensive but better to be on the offensive. If you must get the best out of blogging, you will need to give thoughts to whatever you write before going ahead to make it public.

Although a lot of people who blog already or are trying to go into blogging are not aware, there is a code of ethics for bloggers.

Even if not all bloggers follow this, a code of ethics does exist. While the code of ethics in blogging did not always exist, they came into existence as the blogging sector became more established.

If there is anything that bloggers consider to be of utmost importance, that thing is "transparency." Transparency means a lot to bloggers who adhere to the blogging code of ethics. Let's take a look at transparency in detail.

Sticking to the Truth

Transparency can be looked at as being honest with who you are on your blog, why you have a blog, and what you aim to achieve with your blog.

While being honest is important, it does not mean you should put up details about your life that you are not very comfortable sharing with total strangers.

What it simply means is, if you must put up a piece of information, that piece of information has to be true.

Accepting and Admitting Mistakes

Making mistakes is part of being human. In the course of blogging, errors tend to occur. It does not matter what the reason for your mistake is.

What matters is how you react after making a mistake.

In the world of blogging, when you make a mistake, you should be bold enough to apologize if apologies will make any corrections.

Keeping Up with a Conversation

When blogging, you have to be aware of the presence of comments from your readers. Also, as a blogger, you should not just stop at being aware of comments; you should also respond appropriately.

While blogging means a lot of things to various people, blogging at the deepest level involves a series of communication between lots of people.

Included in these are the blog owner, as well as readers of such a blog.

How to Remain Truthful

Honesty might have just one meaning when it is looked up in the dictionary. However, when it comes to blogging, honesty is not the same thing as it is in advertising or journalism.

The reason for this is the complexity associated with who a person is online. With this in mind, you should give attention to the following:

Blogging Anonymously

There is nothing wrong with making use of a pen name while blogging. Due to the level of honesty that is associated with blogging, especially if the blog is a personal one, lots of bloggers make use of pen names.

This is even more pronounced if the topic under discussion is sensitive.

Being anonymous is not always welcome in the blogging world, so if you decide to be anonymous, it might not remain that way.

After being unknown for a while, your very existence might be challenged by people that follow your blog. This might lead to your identity being made public.

If you come across a situation like this, do not hesitate to be on the defensive.

Paid Posts

Bloggers write reviews for certain products after being paid by the manufacturers of such products.

While this can be looked at as a way for bloggers to earn an income from the work they put into the creation of content, a lot of people in the blogging world consider it an offense when bloggers get paid to write a review about a product without making it known that they were paid to do so.

Appearing as a Fictional Character

This method of writing blogs is one that a good deal of success can be attributed to. While this method is successful, it is associated with a lot of criticism.

When looking to stay honest with your blog, there are specific rules that you need to stick to. Some of these rules include the following:

1. Let your readers know the reason you decided to start a blog and who you are.

2. If for any reason you want to keep your identity and the identities of people mentioned in your blog anonymous, always make it known that you are protecting some identities.

In addition to making people know you are protecting someone, give them the reason for doing so.

3. If for any reason you decide to create a fake blog, you will be doing yourself as well as your readers a lot of good by clearly stating that the blog is fake.

While people can spot a fake blog, making it known that a blog is fake won't put you in harm's way.

4. Once your blog posts begin generating money, you should let those who follow your blog understand the arrangements that are responsible for this income.

Furthermore, you should let them know what way the money you are making from your blog is influencing the content of your blog.

5. If for whatever reason you have to talk about a story or the fact that you did not generate, your readers must get to know what the source of the fact or story is.

In addition to telling your readers what the source of a story or fact is, it will be great if you can put up a link that directs people to the source of the fact.

Always make it a point of duty to observe copyrights. Observing copyrights means you should only make use of photographs and graphics that you have full permission to make use of.

6. You have to be responsible for the content of your blog. This should be the case even if you are not the source of content.

7. There are lots of blogs that make use of content and break copyright rules in the process. The fact that these blogs can do this and get away with it does not make it right to violate copyright rules.

The implication of this is that you have to be very careful when making use of an image without crediting the source of such an image.

Keeping Your Reputation and Privacy Protected

You must be careful about what you post on your blog. When you put up a post on your blog, that post might seem irrelevant after a while. It, however, will remain in existence for long. This is one reason you should not put up a post that can be used against you in the nearest future.

Not everyone who goes through your blog likes you, so to make sure that you do not allow anyone to hurt you, details that make it possible for random people to identify you should not be exposed online.

Doing this could lead to physical confrontation or identity theft. If you are not sure of the details you should not put up them online, some of these details are passwords, social security number, bank account number, your mother's maiden name, place of birth, birthday, and home address.

There are more details that you should not put online.

However, if you can keep the above mentioned details from the eyes of the public, there will be a reduced likelihood of you being a victim of identity theft.

While the details mentioned above are some of the details about yourself that you should keep private, it is equally important that you do not reveal these details about the people you mention in your blog.

If you are not sure how to keep your privacy protected, you can do what lots of bloggers do. You can decide to make use of a handle or stay anonymous.

It is not enough to try to keep your privacy protected on your blog alone. You should be intentional about not leaving any traces between your blog and your social media accounts.

This implies that if you must share the posts you put up on your blog on your social media accounts, you will have to open new social media accounts just for the sake of your blog.

Anonymity is a tool that bloggers can depend on to stay protected. While anonymity can protect you on your blog, it cannot keep you protected when on another person's blog.

This implies that to remain genuinely protected, you will need more than just anonymity on your blog. You will need to come into agreement with people in your sphere of contact that have blogs.

This agreement should include topics that should not make it to their blogs. If this agreement works, you should be able to make the same sacrifice for them.

Chapter 3: Creating Your Blog

Creating a Blogger Blog

If you have never tried blogging but have decided to give blogging a shot, Blogger is the best platform to get started. Blogger is user-friendly, fast, and free. You do not need to be an expert at blogging to make use of Blogger.

This implies that with the availability of Blogger, you do not need to put in a lot of money and get involved in complex installation procedures before discovering how to get the best out of blogging.

On Blogger, all you need to start blogging is to adhere to three simple steps. Below are the steps:

- Open an account.
- Give your blog a name.
- Select a suitable template.

There are lots of hosted blog software platforms. Each of these platforms functions differently. However, all blogging platforms can only be used after you upload specific details. These details are the name of your blog, as well as your contact details.

How to Create an Account

You will be unable to make use of Blogger if you do not have an account. This, therefore, makes owning a Google account the first thing that everyone who is interested in blogging with Blogger has to own. Once you own a Google account, you are ready to create a Blogger blog. To do so, follow the steps below:

1. Go to www.blogger.com.

2. An arrow will appear on the left; click on it.

3. Pick the New Blog option.

4. Choose a name for your blog.

5. Select a URL or blog address.

6. Pick a template: While creating a blog, you will have to choose a template style. This template style can be altered much later.

7. Select the Create Blog option to complete: As soon as this is done, your blog gets established. After ultimately setting up a blog, when the time comes to making a post, you do not have to go through a long process. All you need to do is to log-in and create a post.

Making Use of the Dashboard

As soon as your blog is ready, it becomes a part of a dashboard, which houses all your blogs. With the dashboard, you can easily carry out your blogging duties without going through an entire process.

When looking to write a new post, all you need to do is select the orange-pencil button that is close to your blog's name. If you want to see your blog through the eyes of visitors, click on the "View blog button."

If you want to take a look at the posts you put up in the past, your stats, comments on your blog, details about blog earnings, template, blog setting, and layout, you can get all these by selecting the arrow that is associated with the Posts drop-down list.

Using WordPress

Deciding on Either WordPress.org or WordPress.com

There are certain blog software applications that give bloggers the option of downloading and installing blog software or working with an already hosted service. One of these blog software applications is WordPress.

WordPress.org and WordPress.com can both be used without paying any fee. WordpRess.com, however, is more considered mainstream.

It makes it a lot easier for bloggers to create blogs. It also features tools that bloggers can use to maintain their blogs very easily.

Getting WordPress Installed

This chapter is all about the process that is involved in installing and making use of WordPress. If you are looking to make use of the hosted version, all you need to do is visit www.wordpress.com and follow the instructions you come across.

There are no difficulties associated with installing and making use of WordPress. However, if you must have a smooth sail, you will need to follow certain vital steps.

Registering a Domain

If you want to have total control of your blog, you will need to have a domain. As soon as you select a blog name, the next thing you need to do is buy a domain.

What is a domain? A domain is your blog's brand, web address, and name.

From your domain, visitors can have a clue of what niche your blog is in and what your focus as a blogger is. There are lots of ways to select the right blog name.

However, to choose a name that is still available, you have to take a look at the works of other bloggers.

Choosing a Web Hosting Service

As soon as you pick a domain that is suitable for your blog, the installed WordPress will have to be housed somewhere. There are various ways to select a host.

One of those ways is to talk to people who have been blogging before you. Ask them about the hosts they make use of and what they have experienced making use of such host.

Some technical requirements are needed to work with WordPress. Some of them include the following:

- MySQL 5.6 or greater

- PHP 5.6 or greater

- The mod-rewrite Apache module

The configurations of lots of web hosts have some similarities. Also, irrespective of what your needs are, you can make use of them. However, if you need to know more about WordPress requirements, this page

http://wordpress.rg/about/requirements, can be helpful. That's not all. On WordPress, there are texts you can copy. Once copied, you can send these texts to prospective web hosts. This way, you can find out if the services that they offer are good enough for WordPress.

While the web hosting field is subject to change because of the emergence of new firms on the scene from time to time, certain firms already have a reputation for making all that is needed to work with WordPress available. Below are some of these firms:

- 1&1

- Bluehost

- GoDaddy

- DreamHost

- Media Temple

- HostGator
- SiteGround

If you are looking to get web hosting of outstanding quality, you can depend on the firms already mentioned above. However, if you are looking to work with something new, it is okay to find out what fellow bloggers use.

Microblogging with Tumblr

Tumblr is unarguably one of the most popular microblogging platforms. To make use of this platform, all you need to do is to visit wwww.tumblr.com to begin.

A domain name and web hosting are not requirements.

To get started with Tumblr, stick to the steps below:

- Visit www.tumblr.com.
- Fill in your email address.
- Select a password and type it in.
- Select a username.
- This is the point where you select the Sign Up button.
- Provide details such as age, and click the space provided for accepting the Tumblr terms of service.
- Click the space for verifying that you are human.

Creating a Text Post

On Tumblr, you can create blog posts through the use of links, video, audio files, quotes, photos, and chat excerpts.

To create a post on Tumblr, follow the steps below:

- Select the Text Post icon.
- Select a title for your blog post.
- Fill in the text that makes up your blog post.

As soon as you are done following these procedures, all you need to do is click on "Publish" to make a post. If you do not want to make a post immediately, you can make your post a little more attractive.

How to Format Your Blog Post

On Tumblr, bloggers have the freedom to format a blog post while they are still creating it. The icon for formatting a blog post is positioned just over the content field.

To format a blog post, simply highlight a content. On Tumblr, you can easily experience the effect on making use of an icon just after using it because this platform makes use of WYSIWYG (what you see is what you get).

There are lots of tools that are available for use on Tumblr. Let's get to know what some of them are.

Unordered List

As far as web browsers are concerned, unordered lists usually get displayed as bulleted lists. To make use of the unordered list, type in the items that make up the lists on different lines. This should be one item for a line.

Once done, select all the typed items. After choosing these items, select "Unordered List."

Ordered List

As far as web browsers are concerned, ordered lists have the appearance of numbered lists. To make use of this tool, you do not need to do so much. All you have to do is type in all the items that make up this list into different lines.

Once you are done typing them, select them, and click "Ordered List."

Insert/Edit Link

This is a fantastic tool that can be used to shed more light on a word or phrase in your posts. This tool is used to make any text or image on your bog clickable.

It, therefore, is the tool to make use of if you are trying to direct your audience to a particular site from your blog.

Heading

This is used to change the size of your text. If you are trying to make a subheading in your post have a more legible appearance without changing its fonts, you can rely on heading to make this possible.

Strikethrough

This is used to make corrections.

Italic

This tool can be used to convert any text in your post to italics. To make use of it, all you need to do is select the text you want to italicize and click on italics. Once done, the selected text will be converted to italics.

Bold

This tool is straightforward to use. To make use of it, all you have to do is select the text you want to make bold and click on bold. Once you get this done, the selected text will have a bold appearance.

How to Add an Image to Your Post

Images give life to blog posts. To add a photo to your post on Tumblr, you can select an image on your PC. To do this, all you need to do is select the plus sign that is located close to Text Post window.

How to Add Links to Your Post

When you add links to your post, you increase their value. This is because it makes it possible for readers to know a lot more about the idea being discussed. To add a link to a post on Tumblr, follow the steps below:

- Click a text in your post.
- Select the link tool.
- Type in a URL into the space provided.
- Click on "Done."

Publishing a Post on Tumblr

As soon as a blog post is ready, the next thing to be done is to publish it. To publish a post, you need to click on "Post," and your audience will be able to view your posts.

If you do not want to publish your post immediately, select the Publish drop-down list.

Creating Non-Text Tumblr Posts

You do not need to be a writer to make use of Tumblr. On Tumblr, you can create content that does not require any writing skills.

On Tumblr, you can choose the type of post you want to put up. Here are the alternatives open to everyone who wants to post on Tumblr:

Video

Do you feel like telling the world something but you do not want to go through the process of typing? If yes, this type of post is one you can take advantage of.

This is, however, only ideal if you are not trying to conceal your identity. If you do not want to type but want to hide your identity, this type of post is not one you should make use of.

Chat

The name of this type of post can be quite deceptive. Although it is known as chat, it is not a medium for various people to get involved in a conversation.

If "chat" is not a post type where multiple people on Tumblr can get involved in a conversation, what is it then?

This post type is simply a medium where you can let the world know of a chat you had on another platform. To make use of it, you need to copy and paste.

Audio

Do you want to tell the world something without typing it and also without revealing your identity? This is the ideal post to make use of.

Link

On Tumblr, you do not have to type. Also, there are no rules that state you have to put up content. You can simply decide to share a link. If sharing a link is the way you want to express yourself on Tumblr, "Link" is the way you should make a post.

Quote

Are you interested in sharing a quote either from a book you read or from your favorite author, etc.? "Quote" is the perfect way for you to make a post.

Photo

A picture, they say, is worth a thousand words. Tumblr is very aware of this. Due to this, you can share a picture on Tumblr without attaching any text to it. This form of putting up posts is one that every photographer will benefit a lot from.

Text

This is said to be the traditional way of putting up posts on Tumblr. Putting up texts on Tumblr is not different from doing so with on other blogging platforms.

With all the available ways to put up a post on Tumblr, there are no limitations to how you can express yourself on this blogging platform. This is, perhaps, one way Tumblr stands out from other blogging platforms.

While the already written ways through which bloggers can put up posts on Tumblr are amazing, there is one more. Tumblr offers you the privilege of making use of other bloggers' content. This is possible because of the existence of reblogging.

On Tumblr, there is a button known as Reblog. This button is located at the lower right-hand corner of your blog. It is a button that you can use to put up a post that you came across on another blog on Tumblr.

With this, the next time you come across a post that you like on another blog on Tumblr, all you need is to click on Reblog to get such content to your blog.

How to Customize Your Blog

This process is for bloggers on the WordPress platform. You can give your blog a personality by customizing it. To get your blog customized, click on its avatar.

This is located on the left-hand side of the post creation icon. Once you get your blog to a mode where you can do some editing, some of the things that you can do to alter your blog's appearance are as follows:

- Change the background color of every single post you make on your blog.

- Make your blog avatar invisible or change its appearance.

- Alter your Tumblr blog's accent color.

Configuring Your Settings

Apart from generally customizing your blog, you can also customize your settings. To do this, select the person icon that is located on your Tumblr dashboard.

Once done, go on and click on the gear icon.

Here are some of the settings that can be altered:

- Password: Alter the password that is needed to have access to your blog.

- Email: Alter the email you used in creating your blog.

- Language: Choose the language of your choice for your blog

- Dial-a-post section: Ensure that your account is linked to a phone number.

How to Alter the Appearance of Your Blog

There are lots of advantages to owning a WordPress blog. As the owner of a WordPress blog, you can access lots of plugins and themes. While plugins make your blog more functional, themes change the appearance of your blog.

Every WordPress blog comes with a theme. This theme could either be the theme you chose while setting up your blog or the regular WordPress theme.

How to Locate More WordPress Themes

To locate more WordPress themes for your blog, you should head to choose a WordPress theme. At this point, it is up to you to select between premium and free themes.

While these two types of themes have lots of similarities, premium themes are more detailed in their features and designs.

If you are looking to get free themes, head to the official WordPress.org theme directory. You can also rely on Just Free Themes.

When looking to locate premium themes, your search has to be more detailed. There are various ways to carry out your search. Some of those ways are with the use of the following:

- ThemeIsle
- ThemeForest
- StudioPress

How to Install a WordPress Theme

It is one thing to locate a theme you love and another to make use of that theme. As soon as you discover a theme you want to make use of, you can make use of WordPress in making such theme a part of your site. To get this done, follow the steps below:

1. Go to Appearance.
2. Choose Themes.
3. Select "Add New."
4. If you selected a free theme on WordPres.org, locate the theme and install it. However, if you bought a premium theme, select "Upload Theme." Once done, go ahead to upload the ZIP file gotten from the purchase of the theme.

Your theme will remain inactive on your site even after it gets installed. So to make it active, select "Activate."

How to Add More Customization to Your WordPress Theme

You can make use of WordPress customizer if you are interested in making your theme further customized. This way, you can make striking changes even if you have no idea of coding.

To further customize your theme, head to Appearance and then Customize.

Various themes have various options. So the alternatives that will be available depend on the theme selected. Although there are different alternatives to different themes, there are specific alternatives that are general to all themes. These alternatives are as follows:

- Making changes go live through the use of the Save and Publish
- Making use of the options on the left to make changes
- Making use of the website preview, which is located at the right, to spot a preview in real-time

Adding Functionality to Your Blog

As already stated above, themes are different from plugins. Unlike themes, which are all about the appearance of your blog, plugins are about functionality.

With a new WordPress blog, all you really will be able to do is create pages and put up posts. However, as you get plugins, you will be able to do a lot more with your blog. With plugins, you can enjoy various new functionalities, such as the following:

- Better SEO
- Backups
- Contact forms
- Social network buttons

There are lots of things you can do with your blog. However, to enjoy your blog to the fullest, you will have to rely on plugins. On WordPress, bloggers can access more than 50,000 free plugins.

The implication of this is that there is a plugin for any feature you can conceive in your mind. If you do not want to make use of free plugins, you can have access to premium plugins running in their thousands.

Where to Get WordPress Plugins

To get the best out of your blog, you must be fully aware of how to get both free and paid plugins.

There are lots of places to get both free and paid plugins. However, some of these places are more trustworthy than others. If you are interested in getting free plugins, you cannot go wrong by checking the official WordPreess.org plugin directory.

Unlike free plugins, you cannot rely on the official WordPress.org plugin directory for premium plugins. If you are looking to make use of premium plugins, the most trusted way to get this done is by searching for the plugin you are looking for on Google.

As soon as you locate the plugin you are looking for to make use of, the next step will be to purchase this plugin from a developer with a good reputation.

Plugins That Are Needed by All Sites

In the world of plugins, you can get various plugins for various purposes. There are, however, particular plugins that every site has to make use of. As a blogger, you might know the plugins you need for specific purposes.

You, however, might not be aware of specific plugins that will go a long way in making your job easier. As a website owner or blogger, below are some plugins that you should have:

- Optimole

- WPForms

- Yoast SEO

- WP Super Cache

- Wordfence Security

- Jetpack by WordPress.com

- UpdraftPlus WordPress Backup Plugin

- Google Analytics for WordPress by MonsterInsights

- Social Media Share Buttons & Analytics

How to Install WordPress Plugins

To install WordPress plugins rapidly, I have put down a simple guide. This guide is in simple steps:

1. Head to Plugins and then to Add New.

2. Once at Add New, if you select a free plugin, go ahead and search for that plugin by its name. Once you find it, the next thing to be done is to select Install Now.

3. If you are making use of a premium plugin and not a free plugin, select the Upload Plugin button. Once done, go ahead to upload the ZIP file containing the premium plugin.

After installing the plugin, it will be useless unless it gets activated. In addition to making use of new plugins, to manage the plugins you already own, head to the Plugins tab.

What Is the Next Step after Creating a WordPress Blog?

After successfully creating a WordPress blog, going ahead to personalize it by installing a customized theme, and finally making it a little more functional with the use of plugins, what is the next step to be taken?

A lot of bloggers ask this question frequently. If you are one of them, sit tight and go with the flow.

After owning a blog, personalizing your theme, and getting plugins, there are a lot of things you can do. However, if you will follow in the footsteps of the average blogger, your aim at this point will be to get an increased number of people to visit your blog daily and try to earn some money from your blog.

In addition to getting lots of people to visit your blog and making some money from your blog, you might want to know more about things you actually should have learned before going on creating a blog. Furthermore, you might want to find ways of coming up with catchy blog posts and strategies to make your blog grow.

How to Name Your Blog

It is not enough to name your blog. Whatever name you give to your blog has to be associated with the niche your blog falls into. While this is the norm, if you are merely test-running, you can make use of just any name.

It is, however, vital that you select a name that you won't forget.

There are specific tips that you should follow when naming your blog. These include the following:

Make It Short

The right blog name should be short, easy to remember or spell. It also pays to have something catchy as your blog name.

These are some of the basic criteria that your blog name should meet before you adopt it. This is what makes it possible for your target audience to find you on the internet without much stress.

The idea of having a short blog name also has an impact on your posts. The title of a post on a platform like WordPress usually consists of the blog name. This implies that a long blog name will make it difficult for proper SEO.

Using Your Name Isn't Always the Best

Building a personal blog can give you the idea of choosing your name as your blog name. You must not get carried away. You must think long-term when building a blog.

Since you are building the blog to monetize it, this is not the best option. Go for the catchy and easily recognizable names.

Don't Let It Be Too Focused

Having a niche in mind is suitable for your blog. Nevertheless, it is crucial that you do not pick a name that focuses solely on this niche. You want to give yourself room to grow into something bigger later.

Special Characters and Numbers Are a No

There are times when using a number is crucial in making your blog name easy to recognize. This is usually after you have built a brand around a specific name. If you have not, do avoid these options.

It is also better to stay away from special characters. These can make your blog name challenging to remember. Hyphens can come in handy when making your blog name easier to read. In cases where it is compulsory you use a hyphen, then search for another name.

Do not Go for Brand Names and Trademarks

Not only do these limit your blog, but you might also get into copyright issues. Large businesses don't care if you have no negative intentions. Avoid these for peace of mind.

Name Generators Can Help

When you are finding it challenging to come up with a cool blog name, then you shouldn't shy away from using a name generator. They might not offer the best blog name, but you can get an idea to use in developing yours.

If you want to find similar words to a work you like, using a thesaurus can also help to achieve your goal. A single word can give you inspiration for a blog name.

Get Ideas from Friends and Family

What are friends for? Seriously, talking to your friends or family members can give you the breakthrough you need when brainstorming for the best blog name. Having more heads brainstorming will yield results you might never come up with on your own.

Selecting an Excellent Top-Level Domain

Top-level domains (TLDs) refer to extensions such as .com, .net, or .org when typing in a website. These are some of the most popular, but they are not the only TLDs available.

Several others may seem more appealing to you, but remember, they are lesser-known for a reason. If there are not a lot of people using them, then it will be difficult for your audience to guess the right TLD of your blog.

Availability of the Domain Name

Finding the right blog name is the first part. Finding the perfect blog name is only possible if the domain name is also available. Always check for the availability of a domain name before making your final decision.

Take Your Time

You must not rush into creating a blog name. You have to take your time to come up with the right one that will last for the long term. There are simple reasons for this.

First, a change in your blog name will mean that you also need to change your domain name. Also, it will cause you to change the name on your social media accounts. This is not a great step when you are finally getting to connect with your audience.

Chapter 4: Blogging with More than Words

Blogging has to do with a lot of written content. However, if you do not add images to blogs, you would be unable to send the information you desire accurately.

With images, you can split blocks of text, enhance readers' engagement, and bolster the message you are trying to send with your content. However, images are broad, and it can be tasking to pick the one that suits your blog post.

This means, before fixing an image in your blog, you need to determine the best option.

Knowing this, we will be focusing on how to use visuals for your blogs and optimize them the right way for the best results. But first, why are images relevant?

Why Should You Use Images in Your Blog?

It is not enough to begin inserting images in your blog. They serve a purpose, and you need to know why they are essential in the first place. You also need to know the role images play in your blogs.

First, images give more life to your posts.

If you write content for readers without any visuals, it can become very boring fast. It takes more time for readers to go through images in comparison to texts.

By adding an image in-between content, you can hold the attention of users and make sure that they remain longer than they usually would have.

However, this is not the only reason you need to use images. People tend to take in the information on images faster than they would do written texts.

For instance, by incorporating the image in your posts, readers can quickly memorize the image. Coupled with the fact that they are already spending longer on your page, the benefits come in two-folds.

When they do leave your page, they get relevant information that makes certain that your blog and brand are always on the top of their minds.

Images can help you to achieve more with less than you would with text, which makes them extremely important.

Now you know how beneficial images are, but this does not mean you should go about attaching just any image you find to your blog. You still need to choose the appropriate images, and we will look into how you can do this in the section below.

How to Choose the Right Images

Before you choose an image for a blog, there are numerous questions you need to consider. Here are some of them:

- What message do you want to pass across?
- Who are your readers?

In choosing an image, you have to go with one that aligns with the information you are sending your users.

You don't want to use an image that has nothing to do with your blog post. Doing this will only puzzle your readers.

Also, you want an image that aligns with your brand. Once you upload an image, your readers should always be able to tell that it comes from you.

By looking at the image you have uploaded on your blog, readers should tell what your blog is about and what it aims to achieve.

Also, if you are not going to be creating your images from scratch, you will need to ensure you are getting them from the right location.

You don't want to use an image that will put you in legal issues with those responsible for creating the images. What's more, make certain that you don't choose images from blogs that are in competition with yours.

If you do so, you may lose your readers to the competing blogs.

As opposed to using copyrighted materials, it is preferable you use materials that fall under the Creative Commons. These are materials you can use for any purpose that is not commercial.

This means that they cannot be used for things that will directly bring you income, like ads. If you want to use them to pass some information on your blog, then you are good to go.

However, if you make the mistake of using an image on a blog that brings in income, it may be classified as commercial usage.

Another great way to make sure that you don't fall into legal problems with images is to use one offered by stock websites. Good examples include Shutterstock and Pixabay.

You can also check out a public domain for images.

However, even though stock images are your best bet, they usually do not have any personality behind them. Many readers can easily tell that you are using stock images and can be discouraging to your users.

Instead of this, if you have the skills and time, one of the best options would be to create images yourself.

This is because there is a higher tendency for readers to share images they have never come across before. By creating an image of your own, you eradicate all of the risks that come with using stock images or Creative Commons.

How to Create Your Images

Like we said earlier, creating images of your own on your blog can be of great benefit to you. However, there are a few things you need to note if you do decide to use this route.

When it comes to using photos of your own, the first step would be to get the appropriate equipment. At this point, you will need to consider investing in a high-quality camera.

Using your mobile phone camera will not get you decent images even though they may seem like a cheaper option, but if your goal is to create images frequently, you cannot do without investing in a solid camera.

Along with a quality camera, great lighting will also be essential.

You will also have to learn a few things about staging, as this can help you develop the kind of quality image you desire.

If you are unable to find a way to get around all of these, you might need to get your images from other locations.

Other ways to create images include the following:

Develop Drawings and Graphics

When trying to incorporate images into your blog, you are not limited to photographs taken by you alone. There are numerous options you can leverage, which range from animation, illustrations, and infographics, to further bolster your message.

All of these may consume a little more time than normal photographs; however, they are well worth the extra effort.

Use Screenshots

There are instances where photographs will be inadequate in helping users understand your posts. This is particularly the case when it has to do with very technical posts.

Even if you may be able to comprehend posts without these screenshots, it will make no sense if your readers are unable to.

So use screenshots to carry them along so that they can have a better idea of what you are implying.

Where You Should Fit in Images

Finding the right images is one step of the puzzle. This is because you still have to determine where you want to place the photos.

There are images that are ideal for your home page, while others will be great as the main highlight of your blog. These images can be incorporated in headers alongside other pages.

However, there are images that you can link with a specific post on your blog.

They are called featured images and are significant to the content they are attached to. Anytime individuals post a link to posts like these, the images will come up as thumbnails.

If you fail to choose an image, it can have a negative impact on the number of views on your post.

A default image is selected at random and used as a thumbnail, and sometimes the image chosen may not portray your brand in the manner you desire.

This makes it extremely important that you choose a thumbnail yourself.

Still, there are several things you need to note when choosing a thumbnail. First, pick one that aligns with the way your blog looks as well as its relevance.

Also, make sure you spread images all around posts and not concentrated them in one spot. In addition to this, you want to go with the most intriguing image at the start of the post.

This will ensure users to remain engaged with your website and the information you are sharing.

Finally, you want to use properly optimized images. The section below will delve into how you can achieve this.

How to Optimize Images

If you want images to have the best results in your blog, there are a few rules that can help you achieve this. Below are a few of them:

Include image alt tags. Many people ignore image alt tags, and this is a huge mistake. Alt tags are texts that you can use to describe your image further.

If the image is unable to load in your browser, the alt tag comes up instead. Besides, it ensures your images are search-engine friendly because the information on alt tags makes it easy for search engines to find your images. In turn, this brings traffic to your website.

Cut down on image size. Large images slow down the load page of your blog. This could result in you losing readers. Instead, focus on uploading compressed videos that still retain the quality.

If a video of 200×200 pixel is adequate, there is no point uploading a 1,000×1,000-pixel image.

Ensure your images are easy to share. With the help of Share buttons, make sure that your readers can easily share your images. Visual social networks like Instagram and Pinterest, are places you want to be.

There are various tools that you can use in attaching these buttons to your blog.

What Is Podcasting?

In simple terms, podcasts are a set of audio files that come in episodes that people can subscribe to for updates. It also gives users the chance to download and listen to these series when they have the opportunity.

All podcast episodes can cover a specific topic or could be a continuation of one broader topic.

You will require an audio file as well as an RSS feed that allows users to subscribe, keep up with, and download new episodes every time they are released.

Why Should Bloggers Use Podcasts?

There is a range of benefits that come from using podcasts on your blog. Some of these benefits include the following:

- Users can listen to the audio in any location, even while driving. This is not the same as texts, which require full concentration.

- It can help you reach an audience that has no interest in reading texts.

- Your audience can consume the content you post with less difficulty.

- Podcasting can be an effective means of directing traffic to your blog.

Lastly, if you do not have as much time to write, talking can be faster and less complex than writing a blog post. However, you need to remember that it takes time to be a successful podcaster. Nonetheless, it is possible to be successful. Below, we will be looking into how you can begin a podcast for your blog.

Starting a Podcast

The first step in starting a podcast, similar to every other strategy you want to implement, is to develop a plan.

Put a Plan in Place for Your Podcast

Since the aim is to start a podcast for your blog, you must have already chosen a niche beforehand. You need to incorporate this niche into your podcast too.

So if your blog is focused on finance, your podcast should be as well.

However, if you have troubles streamlining your podcast to a specific area of your niche, the following questions can help:

- What problems are your listeners dealing with, and which would you love to solve?
- If you have the opportunity, what topics would you gladly speak about for hours?
- What topic can you speak about into the later parts of the night without getting bored?

Once you have successfully figured out all of these, the next step would be to choose a name for your podcast.

Pick a Name

Many newbies to podcasting tend to underestimate the value of a good name. The name you choose for your podcast is one that will be stuck with your brand for a long time to come. It is also a crucial aspect of your brand.

So this means you can't choose something random that does not align with your blog. Instead, choose a name that gives your reader an idea of what your podcast is going to be about.

If you already have a blog name, you can incorporate it into your podcast, but this is not a necessity, as you can also pick something very appealing that will urge readers to check out your podcast.

Regardless of the option that you chose to go with, ensure you add a keyword and description to explain further what your show is about.

An excellent way of choosing a great name is to check out the competition in your niche. This way, you can learn some of the most popular names. When you do, use the information to carve out a name that sells for yourself.

To prevent problems down the road, register the domain name the instant you have successfully decided on a name. This can be a great move if your podcast becomes widely known later on.

The Podcast Format

The episode format is similarly used in a host of podcasts. You can decide to pick a unique format for yourself, but ensure you stick to one when you make a choice. This will ensure every episode in your podcast aligns even if they contain different topics. However, your podcast episode should ideally consist of an introduction, announcement, interview if any, and outro.

There are various formats you can choose for your blog, some of which include the following:

Co-host: This podcast still consists of numerous hosts. The episode could be about you and your host speaking about a specific topic, or you can add interviews to the mix.

Interview: Here, it is between you and a guest. It involves you having to ask them relevant questions on a given topic. Any guest you invite should be a specialist on the subject matter being discussed. This subject could be something under your niche that your listeners can get value from.

Solo podcasts: In this form of podcast, you handle the episode on your own. It could involve you teaching your audience something important about a specific topic.

Length of Episode

This is dependent on the kind of content you want to produce. However, if you have nothing valuable to share, be sure to keep it brief. You do not want to fill your episode up with irrelevant materials that give the audience no value whatsoever. Doing this is one of the easiest ways to lose listeners. The episode length is dependent on you, but it is commonly around 20–40 minutes per episode. Whatever option you decide to go with, make sure the content remains relevant.

Release Schedule

Your release frequency is also of vital importance. If you decide to release new episodes twice each week, ensure you remain consistent. You are going to lose listeners if you post sporadically and vanish after each release. Your goal should be to ensure that your listeners can know when to expect new releases from you. This way, they can tune in even before you release a podcast.

Pick a feasible timing and continue to release new podcasts following the schedule you have put in place. However, do not release irrelevant or low-quality materials in a bid to maintain frequency. It will backfire eventually.

Get the Fundamentals Ready

There are a few things you will need to have in place for your podcast. We will be looking into them below.

Podcast artwork: The artwork you choose for your podcast is also of utmost importance. It goes alongside your podcast and should be given the same level of importance. It is one of the first things readers spot when they come across your podcast. This means it needs to be appealing enough to draw the attention of your users when they see your podcast.

Also, ensure that your podcast still looks appealing even when compressed. This is because many podcast lists on iTunes use smaller versions of the podcast art you select. You do not want to choose an image that would be impossible to recognize when shrunk down.

When choosing artwork for your podcast, take note of the following:

- It needs to be identifiable when compressed.
- It should align with your podcast and blog.
- Stay away from extremely long podcast names. It should also be easy to read.

If you do not have any design skills of your own, an excellent way to get good designs for your podcast artwork will be to get the help of freelancers. You can find an array of freelance designers offering this service on platforms like Upwork and Fiverr for a reasonable fee. Another excellent way of creating good artwork is to use Canvas.

Get Your Equipment in Order

To begin a podcast, you need the right set of equipment, and the great news is that it does not have to be extremely expensive. The first and most important equipment you will need is a good computer.

Choosing Music

Incorporating music to your podcasts can help increase its sound more refined. When searching for music to use, make sure you go with those that are royalty-free. This will ensure you do not run into problems down the road.

If you are a great singer, an excellent choice would be to do your recording. Doing this also makes it feel more unique. There is also a range of websites that you can choose royalty-free music from, like Music Bakery.

Go through the uploads and pick one that suits you. The best places to include the music are the intro and outro.

Uploading Your Podcast

Once you are through with your podcast, you will have to host your media files somewhere. You have a broad range of options here, and here are some of the most common ones:

- SoundCloud
- Fireside
- Podomatic

SoundCloud offers you a great price as a starter. It also comes with a media player and lets you publicly upload your podcasts. It also gives you an easy way to incorporate your podcasts to your website.

If you are looking for an all-in-one option, it is the way to go. However, if you want other options, there are many others to pick from.

1. Computer: Obviously, a laptop would be one of the first things to get in place. This is where most of the work will take place right from the recording to the editing. You do not need an excessively expensive one as you can manage with what you already have.

2. Microphone: There are various types of mics with exceptional audio quality you can choose from. If you do not want to spend too much, you can go with a USB microphone. These mics go straight into your USB port and give you the chance to record with ease.

Before you make a purchase, make sure that you go through reviews from past clients online to find out if the mic will suit your requirements.

Other necessary tools include the following:

- Pop filters
- Mic stands
- Headphone amplifiers
- Cable
- Mixer
- Audio interface
- Storage devices

All of this equipment comes in different grades and prices. Create a budget and purchase those that align with it. You do not have to go overboard when buying equipment unless you can afford it. Many of the high-quality equipment comes at a costly price, but there are cheaper alternatives that can also provide you quality output.

Recording and Editing Software

In addition to your tools above, you will need software for editing and recording to develop a good podcast. However, the kind of software you choose is dependent on your technical expertise and budget.

There are various software packages that can help you in these areas. But some of the most common options that offer you both functionalities in one like Logic Pro, Garageband, Audacity, among others.

Audacity is an audio recorder and editor that is very popular and used broadly among podcasters. It is an excellent option if you want something that offers you great functionality at no cost.

It provides you with all of the tools you require to record, edit, and even publish your episodes.

Garageband is also a great option, but in comparison to Audacity, the offerings are not as much.

For those who want in-depth editing, Adobe Audition is the way to go. If you already have the technical expertise, this is undoubtedly a great option. However, it might not be so great if you are new to editing because it will need time to understand and learn.

Uploading to iTunes

There is a range of directories where you can upload your podcasts, but iTunes is where you want to be listed. To do this, follow the steps below:

1. Make sure that all of the information used in your podcast is accurate. These consist of your cover art, title, author name, and description.

2. Once you have confirmed the accuracy of the information, open iTunes and head to the iTunes store.

3. Next, from the right menu, select "Submit a Podcast."

4. After clicking on Submit, log on to iTunes Connect and paste in your feed.

5. Lastly, select Continue, and review the information once more before making the final submission.

Optimize Your Episode Description and Titles

For each of your podcast episode, you will want to make sure that you develop an intriguing description and title. Let it be centered on the benefits listeners stand to gain from your episode.

Also, ensure you include the right set of keywords in your description and a title too. This way, your episodes will show up in the results if anyone runs a search on iTunes individual podcasts.

Promoting Your Blog's Podcast

Similar to writing blog posts, if you don't promote your content, you are not going to be getting any visitor.

This is the same with podcasts as well. If your podcast is exceptionally engaging but listeners don't know it exists in the first place, no one will ever find out how appealing it is.

To ensure that the right number of people you want to listen to your podcasts are listening, you will want to pay attention to promotion.

The following are some of the ways you can promote your podcasts:

Get Help from Other Podcasters

Before you decided to begin podcasting, there were already individuals who picked up the mantle and had gotten proficient at it. There are likely a good number of them in your selected niche. Do all you can to ensure these top podcasters notice you, and who knows, they may help you with promotion. This is the case, especially if you do the same.

Use Your Mailing List

Since you already have a blog, there is a huge chance that you have a mailing list too. Promote the podcast on your mailing list to pique the interest of your readers. There is a huge chance that many of your blog followers would also be interested in listening to your podcast too.

By using your mailing list, you can let them know about the existence of your new podcast episodes and urge them to listen.

Pay for Mentions

There are numerous podcasts in search of people to advertise on their platforms, especially those who are just starting out. This is a very effective and budget-friendly way of advertising.

If you have the financial capacity, you can choose to go with the big names instead. Getting someone established to mention you on their podcasts is an excellent way of getting your podcast out there.

Request Friends to Leave Reviews

Getting reviews is an excellent way of getting exposure for your podcast. After you have published and uploaded your podcast on iTunes, reach out to your loved ones and friends, and ask them to give you a review.

If you get a good number of reviews in the first hours after you upload an episode, you could be moved to the New and Noteworthy section on iTunes, which is a remarkable way to gain exposure.

Remain Consistent

Like we stated earlier, achieving success as a podcaster is not something that happens overnight. You won't become one of the top podcasters with millions of downloads after a few episodes.

You have to be realistic in your quest. It takes time to create a vast audience base anywhere, including podcasts.

Because the first set of episodes you published did not pan out as you desired does not mean the next step is to quit.

Instead, be sure to post episodes regularly using your stipulated posting schedule.

Also, remember that you need to improve on quality as you move. This way, your audience base will grow to the height you desire.

Wrap Up

Podcasting offers you a great chance to develop your network and build better relationships with your audience. It can be of great benefit to your blog or brand in the long run.

Chapter 5: Promoting Your Blog

In promoting your blog, there are several options available to you. That means you can decide on what route to take in your blog promotion. Taking a route doesn't imply choosing a single option.

To effectively promote your blog to your audience, you must implement multiple options. This will ease the process of reaching a large number of your target audience.

Here is a look at some of the best options available to you.

Networking

Most times, interacting with other bloggers will give you access to all the information you need to for improvements on your blog. These include the best ways to promote the blog. To meet with these bloggers, you must be willing to network.

Networking allows you to connect with people in the same profession that understand you better.

You must meet with other bloggers to build a genuine relationship. It is easy to meet people to exploit them for your gains, but this won't get you far.

If someone sees you as a true friend, they are sure to notice when you are merely trying to take advantage of them. There are blog conferences where you can network with other individuals.

Guest Posting

Guest posting is an action that involves writing content to publish it on the blog or website of another individual. These blogs or websites on which you post content are those with an audience that you wish to reach with your content.

It is an excellent means through which you can connect to new users that can become regular visitors on your blog.

There are several other reasons why you need to include guest posting in your strategy to grow your blog. The first is that it assists you in developing a better professional relationship with other bloggers.

These relationships also offer influence in creating conversions on various social platforms.

Another reason is to improve your rankings on search engine results. This is through the inclusion of a backlink to your blog when you create a guest post on other blogs. Search engines rank blogs with backlinks from other reliable blogs or websites higher on the search results.

Guest post is a way to establish your blog as an authority in the industry. The higher the quality of the guest post content, the more readers you can attract to your blog.

You can get the best results from your guest post if it contains content detailing unique research that you have performed. Remember, it must be content that is relevant to the target audience.

Posting Useful Comments on Other Blogs

Don't mistake this action for guest posting. Here you are merely reading posts on other blogs and posting a comment that you know will be relevant and helpful to the readers of the blog.

In addition to these comments, you can include a URL that redirects traffic to your blog.

The only sure way to get this traffic is to post only when you actually have something meaningful to add to the discussion. A better insight into the topic of the blog post goes a long way.

This will attract readers to open your link to find more information on the subject.

Improving Search Result Rankings and SEO

There are different steps you can take to perform a search engine optimization on your blog. Promoting your blog also means getting it to appear higher up on the search engine results. This is why search engine optimization is essential.

There are various steps that you can take in making this possible. You must go through these steps prior to the date you publish a post on your blog.

This is because most of these steps involve making some minor adjustments to the post. The steps include the following:

- The main headline, H1, of the post, should contain the keyword.
- Avoid creating a post that appears spammy by making the keywords fit in naturally.
- The meta description should contain the keyword.
- Subheadings such as H2, H3, and H4 should include a related keyword.
- Learn how to implement latent semantic indexing (LSI) keywords in your post.
- The page title tag must contain the keyword.
- When comparing the number of each word or terms appearing in the post, the keyword should appear most.

These are just a few tips to help with promoting your blog. You may need to perform more in-depth research into SEO for better results. It is a vast topic.

Another way to improve search result rankings is through the use of the Google XML Sitemap. It is a plugin that WordPress users can quickly access.

This plugin is a means through which you can notify search engines anytime you publish new content on your blog.

To enable search engines (e.g., Yahoo, Google, Ask.com, and Bing) to index new blog posts faster, this plugin develops a sitemap. Another available option is through the use of Ping-O-Matic.

This allows you to notify a specific search engine of your posts. You enter the URL of the post, and it does the rest. These are actions that you can take to yield results much faster.

Include Social Media Sharing Buttons on Your Blog

Most of the members of your audience will have a friend list of users that you cannot reach. Why not let them connect you with these users? That is what the social media sharing buttons on your blog are there for.

After installing these buttons on your page, placement also matters. You want to place them in a position where they are easy to find by your readers. These buttons should be close to the content you want readers to share.

Minimize the number of buttons on the page and remove any form of share count as it can distract your readers from sharing the content.

Repurpose Content

In promoting your blog, it may be beneficial to have other platforms on which you can share your content. An excellent platform for this purpose is YouTube. Considering its ranking as the second largest search engine, you don't want to miss out on the opportunity to connect with new individuals.

So how do you get articles on a platform meant for videos? The only option is to repurpose your articles for this platform. To repurpose your content means to change it into a different format.

In this case, you are changing from plain text to video format. The first step is to create a YouTube channel.

The users you are trying to reach through your YouTube channel are those that prefer visual and audio content over plain texts. These can be exceptionally helpful with how-to guides.

The first step to repurposing content is to determine what content on your blog has the most engagement.

This is a topic that your audience enjoys. You can turn this into video format and post on your YouTube channel. Here, you are promoting the content to a new audience.

You can then add a URL that redirects viewers to your blog in the description of the video. Another option that you can choose is to repurpose content into a podcast. There are lots of people who listen to podcasts.

You want to reach individuals during their commute to work or while they are relaxing. These are periods when audio contents have more advantages.

During the podcast, you can mention the name of your blog for listeners to visit when they have the opportunity.

Visit Up-Vote Communities and Aggregate Sites

An aggregate site is a site that offers information on a particular topic from a diverse number of sources. They usually consist of communities where each of them has a specific interest. You can share your content in this community to reach out to a large number of your target audience.

On these sites, each member has the option to vote. They can vote on any post on the site, and they have the opportunity to select either good or bad. A good is an up-vote, and it shows that your post is valuable. Posts with too many down-votes are regarded as junk.

Promoting Your Blog on Social Media Networks

Social networks provide an opportunity for you to share your blog with your friends and other users on the network. When used in the right manner, a social network is a vital tool for building communities, friendships, and audiences for your blog.

On most blogs you visit, there is usually the option to share a post on various social networks. These options consist of the title of the post in addition to a link to the post.

This is an option that makes it possible for your audience to assist in promoting your blog on their social media channels.

As the blog owner, it is vital that you also take the same step. In promoting your blog on social networks, it is necessary to decide on the right networks to use.

Opening a profile on all the available platforms won't do much good. You need to focus on just a few of these platforms.

When selecting a social network, there are specific questions you can ask yourself. Here is a list of these questions to serve as a guide to choosing the right platform:

- How much time can you invest in social networks?
- Is there a specific social network that is most suited for sharing your type of content?
- Is there a platform that offers functionalities that are beneficial to bloggers?
- What platform has a more significant number of users that fall within your target demographic?
- Are your current audience members active on any social media network?
- What network is most popular with friends and family members?

Answering these questions will help you determine what social platform you should focus on when promoting your blog.

Once you select the right platforms, you have to familiarize yourself with that platform. Depending on how the platform operates, you can classify them.

These include the following:

- Media sharing platforms (e.g., Instagram, YouTube, and Pinterest)
- Friend-based platforms (e.g., Twitter and Facebook)
- Professional platforms (e.g., LinkedIn)
- Informational networks (e.g., StumbleUpon)
- Networks for hobbies (e.g., Last.fm for music and Goodreads for books)

In promoting your blog, you can focus on some of the most popular right now, and they are as follows:

- Facebook
- Twitter
- Instagram
- Pinterest
- LinkedIn

The reason why these platforms are popular is a result of the unique features they offer to their users. As a blogger, you cannot underestimate the amount of traffic you will get from a platform like Facebook. Although a large number of the younger demographic is moving to other platforms, Facebook remains relevant.

To start promoting your blog on social media networks, follow the tips below:

Sharing Snippets of Posts

To build a loyal following on social media networks like Facebook and Twitter, you can start by sharing snippets. These shouldn't include links to make it more natural and appealing to other users.

The snippet should be a part of your post that makes sense when written on its own. In some cases, you can also choose to share some helpful tips that you cannot make into a post.

These are other things you can share to grow your followers and audience.

Promoting on Facebook

To boost your blog on Facebook, you can start by creating a Facebook page for the blog. There should be consistent updates on the Facebook page anytime you post new content on the blog. You should also visit various Facebook groups.

Search for groups that are relevant to your blog niche, join, and make sure to share your blog post with the members of these groups. Some Facebook groups focus on promoting a new post from bloggers.

If you have gone through the process of networking and established excellent relationships with other bloggers, you will find a lot of them on Facebook. You can connect with these bloggers to have them share your post on the Facebook page, group, or profile.

Using Twitter

One of the features on Twitter is the option to build a Twitter list. This allows you to group certain users and separate them from the rest of your followers. You can create a list to identify users that share your posts.

These are the users that will possibly share future posts. You can also reach out to users sharing content similar to yours on the platform. To find these users, you can use a hashtag or type a phrase into the search box.

You can pick out users with a decent number of followers and then click on the Follow button. Reach out to these users through a direct message to know if they would like to read and share your post if they find it valuable.

Remember, anyone who has shared your post in the past is likely to do so in the future. Make sure you alert these users when there is a new post.

Add a Link to Your Blog

Regardless of the social network you use, it is necessary to have a link that redirects users back to your blog on your profile. This is how you can quickly get users to visit your blog.

Some users may see a few posts without a link and want to find out more about what you have to say. Going through your profile is the best way to get the necessary information they need.

Don't Ignore Social Bookmarking Sites

A social bookmarking site offers users the opportunity to bookmark a website to revisit later. The user will also have the option of including a tag when bookmarking the site.

One of the unique features of a social bookmarking site is the opportunity for other internet users to see the website when they search for the tag.

This is why your blog needs to be on these sites. Anyone who has an interest in the content of your blog will be able to find it if they search on the platform.

Search for Forums and Join the Discussion

Depending on the niche of your blog, there will be a forum for you to visit. These forums are excellent places to share your blog posts and attract new readers.

If you have no idea what a forum looks like, then you should look up Quora. It is currently one of the most popular forums on the internet.

It is a platform that allows users to discuss diverse topics. This is an excellent place to start if you want to start attracting users.

The main benefit of a forum that is specific to your niche is the direct access to the target audience that it offers.

Go for Paid Promotion

Free marketing is good, but most of the times, nothing beats paid advertising. There are various paid promotion tactics that you can use in reaching out to your target audience.

You can kick off your paid promotion with Google AdWords since it offers access to a large number of users. Another option is through retargeting.

You may also know this as remarketing. It is a way of reaching out to users who have visited your page at one point or the other. It is a form of advert that follows your users to other websites they open after visiting your site.

Chapter 6: Making Money Blogging

Blogging can be very tasking if there are no rewards for your efforts. Therefore, it is crucial you know how to get rewards for your blogging efforts. These are ways through which you can make money when you remain consistent.

There are various options that you can pick from to earn a steady income. To increase your revenue, you can engage in multiple options.

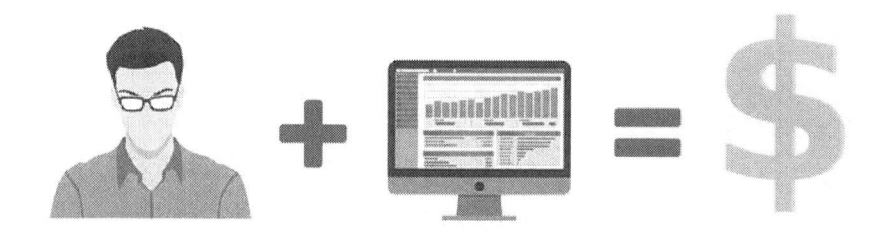

The following are some of the most popular options available.

Affiliate Marketing

Affiliate marketing is a process through which you make money by promoting the products of a person or company in exchange for a commission. The commission is only available if there is a sale from your promotional efforts.

For each sale the company makes, you receive a commission.

One of the enormous benefits of affiliate marketing is the opportunity to build a passive income stream.

First of all, to start making money through affiliate marketing, you have to join an affiliate program. In addition, you also need to select specific products that you will be promoting on your blog.

You must pick products that are relevant to your audience and the content you share on your blog. There are different options available for redirecting traffic to the product page. These include creative copies like banners and text links.

The company usually provides these creative companies to its affiliates to ease the process. You can paste it on any part of the website to redirect members of your audience to the landing page.

You will also get an affiliate code from the company, which is like an identification tag when you refer anyone to the company.

Your goal as an affiliate is simple — marketing. You will find any channel or means you feel will get customers to purchase a product and take advantage of it. In this case, you are taking advantage of the incoming traffic on your blog. These are potential customers that you have a considerable influence over.

You will create content that focuses on the product you want to promote and give reasons why an individual should pick it over others on the market. When engaging in affiliate marketing, you can decide if you want your audience to know or not.

In affiliate marketing, product reviews and comparisons help in driving more sales. Choosing products they are more familiar with and highlighting the key features and differences is crucial.

Amazon Associates is one of the most popular affiliate marketing programs you can join to earn money through your blog.

Creating a Membership Site

This is an area of your blog that you make private with the sole intention of making money off it. This private area is designed in the form of a membership-based forum that requires a subscription from an individual before they are granted access. This area must offer services that are unavailable on the regular blog page to make it worth the money spent.

There are various ways to achieve this. You can start by offering an in-depth look into a particular topic on a blog. Understanding this will need a proper example.

Let's say your blog revolves around reducing environmental pollution. In one of your posts, you can introduce your readers to a simple way to design and build a plastic shredder. The regular blog contains a brief look at the project and nothing more.

On the membership area, you can go further to give details on the size of the cutters, the hopper, the capacity of the gear, materials selection, and much more. The information listed above offers an in-depth look at how you were able to develop your plastic shredder. It simplifies the stress that your readers will go through if they decide to undertake the same project.

Also, you can offer a video tutorial that gives your audience a look at the final product during operation. This is a content that is worth paying for.

You can charge users for daily access to this area of your blog. Do note that this option will not be suitable if you can't come up with high-quality, premium content regularly. Premium content is what makes your blog attractive.

Building up your audience is crucial to the success of this membership site.

Selling Digital Products on Your Blog

Creating digital products is one of the simplest means to make money through blogging. The main reason it remains a profitable option is due to the low money investment requirement that it requires.

Regardless, it often involves a lot of time investment to create a valuable digital product.

In this section, I will be introducing you to three ways to make money from digital products. Read on to find out more about these.

Offering Online Courses

Everyone wants to learn something new. It is best when the learning schedule is flexible. This is what online courses provide.

In your case, the course focuses on your area of expertise. You create a syllabus that covers topics that your audience has an interest in. You can then charge them for access to the information the course provides.

It can sometimes be a challenge to create a course with relevant content on your own. Since you have already established a relationship with your audience, you can ask what they want to know more about. You can then focus on the topics with the highest number of suggestions.

This way, you are creating a course that your audience will have a genuine interest in paying for. To attract people to pay for the course, you can separate it into two categories: the free version and the paid version.

The free version is a basic look at some of the topics and what the course offers. The paid version is a premium version that grants access to the full content of the course as well as personalized support.

Sell E-books

At this point, you should have come across several websites offering e-books for sale. You will often find an advert on the homepage of the website when you visit. There is an opportunity for you to make money through this option.

Creating an e-book can be very easy. You can decide to include some of the best content on the blog while adding unique chapters that will entice your readers. You can then place them on your blog at a price.

The download automatically unlocks once a reader pays the specified amount. Remember, it is crucial your e-book appears appealing to the readers. You need to design a high-quality cover for this purpose.

You can decide to hire a professional to help you with this part or use a tool like Canva. Similarly, you can also get a freelancer to assist in writing the e-book.

I mention this as an option, but if you are currently gaining massive traffic on your blog without outside help, there is no need to use this option.

Webinars

There are certain similarities between a webinar and an online course. The unique difference is that, with most webinars, you can host it live. This means your audience can get the opportunity to ask you questions in real-time.

It is like hosting a question-and-answer session online. You can decide to use your blog in registering participants or host the webinar directly on the blog. Regardless of the option you choose, this is an excellent way to make money from the blog.

Sell Physical Products

Making money through your blog will not be complete without mentioning the option of selling physical products. The products you can sell include merchandise like T-shirts, hoodies, and many more.

If you pick this option, there are several ways you can go about it.

These simplify the process of making sales through physical products. They include the following:

- Creating a dropshipping shop
- Creating an e-commerce website
- Opting for the Amazon Affiliate shop

Offer Paid Consultation

As a blogger with massive traffic to your blog, only means one thing. You have established yourself within your niche. Therefore, you will have part of your audience that is willing to pay for your services.

These services include consultation and coaching services. Consultation services will allow you to share your expertise by providing your client with strategies and advice that they can use in growing their business or blog. There is no investment needed, just the knowledge you have accumulated over the years.

Another area you can work to get money is as a life coach.

A little bit different from consultation, coaching involves you creating goals, offering guidance, and giving advice to your client on how to improve their life.

A little out of your league? Don't fret. People are looking for a coach in different areas. Some people want a blog coach while others want writing coaches.

The success of your blog is proof that you will fit it excellently.

Remember, you need to show that you are passionate about a specific topic and also knowledgeable. This is the essence of having a niche for your blog.

Pay-Per-Click Advertising (PPC)

One of the most popular models for advertising online is the PPC model. This allows an advertiser to pay for every click on their advert. You can start placing these adverts by joining a PPC ad network. A popular PPC ad network for most bloggers is Google AdSense.

Using Google AdSense

You are currently getting reasonable traffic to your site. The question, what is an easy way to make money from this traffic? The simple answer is Google AdSense.

This is a viable option before you start, including other options like online courses and e-books into the mix.

Google AdSense is a program from Google that allows you to display adverts on your blog and videos with the possibility of earning money from these adverts.

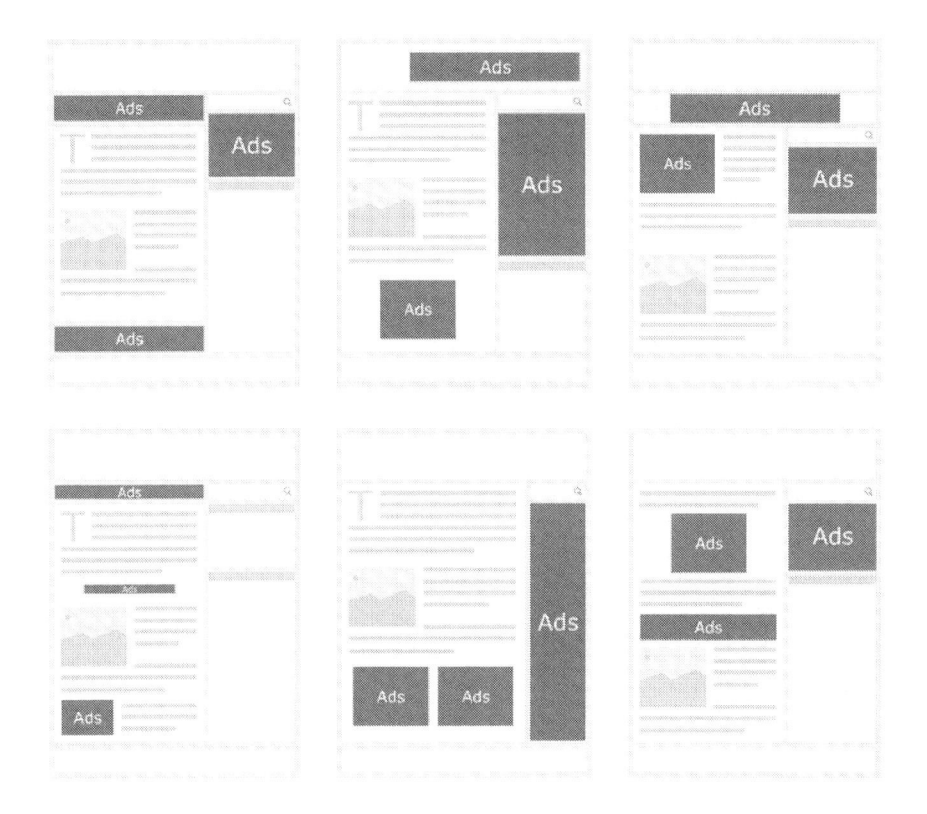

To make money, visitors and readers on your website must click on the ads. To display these ads, all you need to do is include a line of code on your blog.

Google AdSense differs from other forms of online ads since the only action you need to take after adding the line of code is to keep traffic coming to your site. That means consistently publishing excellent content.

There are several benefits of Google AdSense. First, it is free and easy to join, giving you quick access to a means to make money through your blog. Another benefit is the opportunity to connect a single account to multiple websites or blogs. It offers various ad options for you to pick one that will be suitable for the design of your website.

In addition to these benefits, it also has some demerits. The first is the possibility of losing your account quickly. There are rules and guidelines for using the Google AdSense, and any breach will lead to a loss of the account.

Another issue with Google AdSense is how it operates. The ads require your visitors to click on them, and this will redirect them to another landing page. This means that to earn money, visitors must leave your blog page.

In truth, Google AdSense isn't the best option available for making money through adverts.

There are other ways you can make money from ads if you decide to ignore this option. I also forgot to mention that you can only receive payment when you reach the $100 threshold of the program.

Sell Your Blog Space to Private Advertisers

If pay-per-click advertising networks aren't bringing you the kind of money you expect, there are other ways to make money through advertising. One of these is to connect directly with the advertiser.

The main benefit of this option is the opportunity to set your rates. That means you determine the exposure that your blog can offer to these advertisers and charge them based on this exposure.

This option is often more profitable than the pay-per-click ads since you make money from the advert appearing on your blog. The advert can appear in the form of a button, link, or banner on your blog.

Private advertisers can decide to contact you directly, or you may need to make the first move to get them on your blog. There is also the option of creating a sponsored post, which we will discuss next.

Sponsored Posts

A sponsored post refers to an article on your blog that you received payment to publish it. This payment can come from a brand, business, or company that has an interest in your audience. Their operations are usually closely related to the niche your blog focuses on.

Depending on the agreement between you and the client, you may need to create the content that you publish for the sponsored post. In other cases, the client may provide the content.

The former will yield higher profits, while the latter will be lower. The format of the sponsored post will vary based on customer requirements.

Some customers want the post to be a product announcement while others want reviews, infographics, or announcement of sales.

A paid blog post review is an excellent option if you are a part of an affiliate program. It means you will be publishing several reviews on your blog regularly. Businesses cherish the form of exposure they can receive from reviews.

For legal reasons, it is necessary to include a statement that tells your audience that it is a sponsored post. It can be at the beginning or at the end of the post. Let the message of the statement be clear to your readers.

Blog Flipping

If you are familiar with websites like Flippa.com, then you will know how easy it is to buy and sell any online business.

Yes, that includes a blog. This is only an option if you consider yourself an expert in creating niche blogs.

You can build up a blog and then sell it on this platform. There are several tasks you must complete for an attractive blog. Anyone buying the blog will be looking for these qualities.

The qualities of an excellent blog include a history of high-quality content, an email list, a large number of readers, and sources of income. The sources of income include the adverts options on the blog.

If you want to go into blog flipping, then you must develop yourself in this area. There is a ton of money to be made from this option. You can also choose to sell your blog later if there is ever a need to leave the blogging profession.

Chapter 7: Promoting Your Blog and Making Money through Email Marketing

What Is Email Marketing?

Email marketing is a marketing strategy that involves creating excellent content that you send to your customers and prospects through an email. These emails can be used to promote your products or services or offer general information that will be relevant to your subscribers.

In monetizing your blog, email marketing is one of the most vital strategies that you must implement. There are numerous benefits that you can enjoy if you decide to adopt email marketing.

Benefits of Email Marketing

It Is Easy to Share

Like content on social media platforms, emails are also easy to share with other individuals. Your customers can decide to do this by forwarding it to members of their email list. This is much easier if you provide high-quality content that they are sure others will want to read.

This is a form of word-of-mouth marketing that can assist in promoting your blog and the products or services you offer.

It Doesn't Interfere with the Activities of Your Subscribers

When marketing, you want to get your message across to your subscribers. At the same time, you don't want to cause any form of interference in their lives that will cause them to boycott your brand.

This is an area in which email marketing has an advantage over other types of marketing like telephone marketing.

With email marketing, your subscribers will view your email at a time when it is convenient. This is great since it makes them more likely to go through the entire content of the email.

It Helps in Focusing on Individuals with Genuine Interest

In a later section, we will discuss more on email lists. This is a list of the subscribers that receive the emails from your email marketing campaign. For an individual's email to appear on this list, it means they have given their permission.

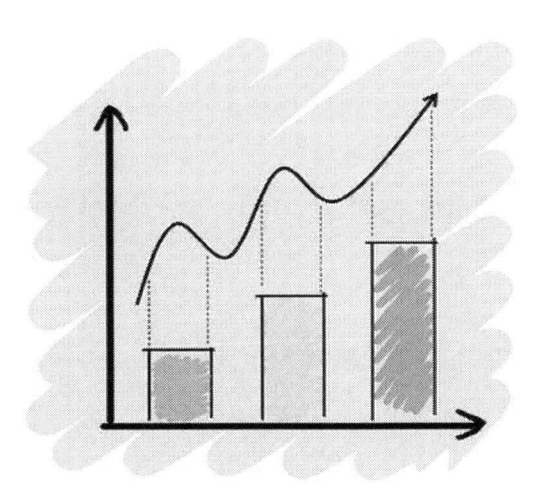

This is an essential benefit of email marketing. Only individuals that have a genuine interest in what you have to offer will give permission to receive emails from you. Also, there is an unsubscribe feature that allows them to revoke these permissions when they lose interest.

You Can Test What Works

Email service providers, the companies that support email marketing, offer a feature known as A/B testing. This feature allows you to send varying forms of an email to test the effectiveness of images, subject lines, email copy, call to action, and other parts of the email. This allows you to create and send one that will get the maximum engagement from subscribers.

It Is a Cost-Effective Marketing Strategy

In comparison to traditional forms of marketing, email marketing is much cheaper. It eliminates the need to provide money to cover the cost of media space, advertising fees, or printing. Besides, most email service providers usually charge based on the number of emails you send.

You Can Measure Performance

Email marketing allows you to measure your performance. This is possible through the use of analytics tools. By monitoring the engagement rate and other metrics of your emails, you can make improvements to enhance your results in later campaigns.

It Helps Save Time

Blogging can take up a lot of your time. This can be an issue if you include the need to engage in various marketing campaigns. Email marketing offers an automation feature that can minimize the amount of work you have to do to ease this stress.

You can set specific actions that visitors take on your blog as triggers for emails to be sent. These emails are prepared beforehand, and they can vary depending on the action the visitor takes.

With so many benefits of email marketing, it is easy to see why you need it in boosting your income from your blog. Nonetheless, there are some issues with email marketing. These include the following:

- Problems with deliverability
- Some users marking your sender name as spam

- Optimization for different platforms

You must overcome these issues and some others when using an email marketing campaign. For a successful email campaign, an email list is essential.

So how do you get one?

Building an Email List

An email list is a list containing the addresses of every user that subscribes to your email marketing campaign. You can choose to build an email list from scratch or choose to buy one.

To get the most out of your campaign, you must be willing to do the work of building an email list from scratch.

Buying an email list involves paying a company for a list of users that you can send your emails to with the hopes of reaching some prospects.

The problem with this option is that multiple users on the list can send a spam complaint against you. Too many complaints and your emails will go directly into the spam folder.

Another issue is that there may be a lot of inactive users or wrong addresses on the list. These can lead to a bounce. A bounce in email marketing occurs when your messages are unable to deliver. It can be either a soft bounce or a hard bounce. Bounce can lead to email services such as Gmail registering your name as spam.

These are some of the reasons why building an email list from scratch is your best option. Two tools that can help you to create an email list are the opt-in form and lead magnet. The quality of the content you post on your blog also plays a crucial role in achieving success.

Let us take a look at lead magnets and opt-in forms in detail for more understanding.

Lead Magnets

Building an email list is possible if you can get users to give you their email addresses. Most users won't give you their email address just because you asked. You have to provide them with something that they will find valuable enough to provide you with the address you need.

This item that you give the user is a lead magnet. You can consider it a form of a bribe that gets you what you need. A lead magnet can be in any form but must be something that the users want.

In most cases, your lead magnet is a digital material that your visitors can get immediately. Another vital quality of the lead magnet is that it is something you create on your own. This makes it unique and worth having to the visitor.

Since they are necessary to convince your visitors, there are other qualities that your lead magnets must possess. These include the following:

1. It must be relevant. An essential quality of any effective lead magnet is the relevance to the visitor. For it to be relevant, your lead magnet must meet a specific need of your visitors. If you know the essential details regarding your target audience, this shouldn't be an issue.

2. It should add something new. There are various things that you can add to your visitors through your lead magnet. This is one of the qualities that makes it valuable. If it offers new information or provides a means to develop a new skill, your visitors will be eager to have it.

3. It shouldn't take a lot of time to go through. Give someone a new skill for free, and they will come back for more. This is what you need to do with a lead magnet. Considering that they only provided their email address and not money for the lead magnet, a prospect will be willing to pay for any additional product you can offer.

To make this possible, you need to make it easy for them to get this skill. That means you have to make the lead magnet easy to consume. If it is an e-book, you must make it short. Anything over 100 pages will make people lose interest quickly.

A lead magnet on your blog can appear as any of the following:

- Webinar
- Spreadsheet
- Quizzes
- E-books
- White papers
- Free trials

- Coupons
- Free consultations
- Templates
- Online course
- Access to a membership site

Opt-In Forms

Now you have the lead magnet in place, but how do you get visitors to go for it? This is where the opt-in form comes in. Using this form, you can add a few lines to make the lead magnet attractive to the visitor.

The lines can include some advantages of the lead magnet to the visitor. These lines should contain information that makes the visitor want to subscribe to see what it truly offers.

To ensure the opt-in form does its job from convincing the visitor to getting them to subscribe, these are some of the essential components that it must possess:

- A headline
- A description
- A simplistic body

- Excellent visuals
- A subscribe button that stands out

After creating an opt-in form that appeals to your visitors, you must install it on your blog. There are different options available to you when installing the form. You can select from any of the following options to install it:

- Using a splash gate
- Installing in a scroll box
- Using an exit-intent popup
- Installing as a floating bar
- Installing as a timed lightbox popup
- Using a welcome gate

There are other options available when deciding on the position of the opt-in form. These options usually involve the opt-in form appearing on the page permanently.

Email List Segmentation

To take your game to the next level with email marketing, you must not overlook the area of email list segmentation. It is a means through which you can engage in targeting during your email campaign.

Email list segmentation is a process or the act of splitting your email list into smaller categories. Certain factors determine the subscribers that will fall into these categories as you break down the email list.

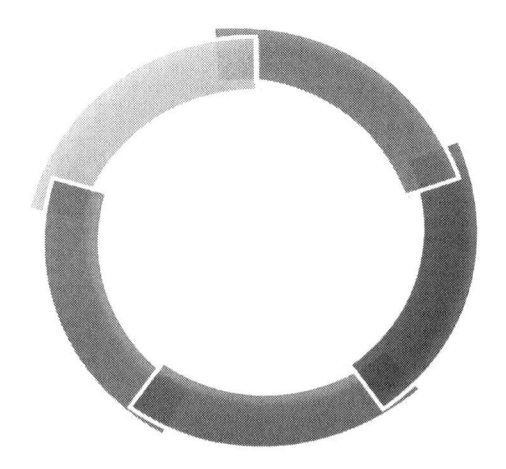

The importance of the email list is to prevent subscribers from receiving emails that won't interest them.

Through the email list segmentation, you can send targeted content to a group of subscribers and increase your chances of generating conversions and getting more profit.

Other benefits of email list segmentation include an increase in the open rates and click-through rates of your email. It also simplifies the process of making use of autoresponders in your email marketing campaign.

In creating email list segments, there are various factors you can use. It is up to you to decide on what factors will be most effective in segmenting your list. The following are some of the common factors in use:

Preferences

Despite the quality of the products you have available, some specific customers don't have an interest. These customers subscribe for the sole reason of getting notifications on new blog posts. Others want to know about any new product you have available.

These are two unique preferences of subscribers. In creating list segments, you can have a segment for updates on new posts and another for product updates.

Open Rate

When segmenting is based on open rates, you are looking to separate your active users from the rest. You can then decide to offer a discount on products or any other incentive to show appreciation to these users.

Lead Magnet

It is common to change your lead magnets quite often. This means that you will have some differences in the lead magnets that users selected. Segmenting your list based on the lead magnet a subscriber selected when opting in the email list helps. You can use this in identifying topics that interest them and the content format they prefer.

Location

Sending an invite to an event in Toronto to a subscriber in New York is not a great idea. For this reason, having email list segments based on the location of your subscribers helps.

Tracking through Google Analytics

Depending on the email service provider you pick, an analytics tool may be available. If you want a free tool that does this and so much more, you must tilt toward the use of Google Analytics.

This is essential for analyzing your performance and determining what went wrong with an email campaign.

Another huge plus is that this is a free tool. It is simple to use and integrate into your email campaign.

Here is a quick look at how to use this powerful tool in boosting sales and promoting your blog through email marketing:

Create Your Goals

There is no way you can accurately assess your performance if you don't have any goal you are working toward. It is necessary to determine if you are meeting up with these goals or not to know if you are performing excellently or not.

This is the first step after signing up and creating a Google Analytics account.

Google Analytics offers three options to users during the goal setup process. These include the following:

- Custom goal
- Goal template
- Smart goal

Depending on the option you select, there are other details that you must add to complete the process. When you complete this, move on to the next step.

Add URLs

Knowing the source of traffic on your blog is vital in determining the performance of your email marketing campaign. Posting a URL is a simple method you can use in redirecting traffic to your blog.

You can post this URL on a social media platform like Twitter or Facebook and also include it in the emails you send to your subscribers.

So how do you know if the traffic your blog is currently generating is through the URL on your social media channels or email? You can do this by including trackable URLs.

These are links that include an Urchin Tracking Module (UTM).

There is an option to use the Google Analytics URL Builder to generate a trackable URL manually. Below is a quick look at the steps you must take to do this:

- Include the website link you want to redirect traffic to.
- Add a campaign source; this is the origin of the visitor, which can be a search engine, a specific email, and so on.
- Include a campaign medium; this is the type of traffic, and it can be email, organic, paid search, referral, or unknown.
- Add the campaign name.

Add the Advanced Segment

This is the option that makes it possible to monitor the behavior of every visitor on your website.

Get Your Reports

For an in-depth analysis of your email marketing performance, Google Analytics provides reports to the users. There are various types of reports, which include the following:

Campaign Report

This is an overall look at the performance of your email marketing campaign or any other campaign you choose to monitor. Some of the details in this report are the number of pages a visitor views, the number of new users at the end of the campaign, the time spent by visitors, and more.

Behavior Flow Report

What is the next action of your visitors after going through your email campaign? What pages do they open as soon as they land on your page? These are some of the questions the behavior flow report helps you answer.

Real-Time Report

This gives you a look at the active users currently on your website who were redirected from an email campaign you set up. Other details include the device they are using in viewing the page, their location, and the page they are currently viewing.

What Can You Sell through an Email Marketing Campaign?

You can sell anything. This includes both digital and physical products. That's why it is a form of marketing.

It allows you to advertise products that you feel will meet the needs of a specific segment of your subscribers.

You can also promote new products by offering discounts and redirecting traffic to the product page on your blog.

In promoting your blog, sending high-quality content to your subscribers can prompt them to share it. If they know that your email will offer value to someone they know, they will be willing to forward.

This is a form of word-of-mouth marketing, and the only difference is that it is happening online.

Chapter 8: How to Form a Blog Monetization Strategy

Your blog monetization consists of the various business aspects of your blog. To create a blog monetization strategy, you need to think like a businessman. Stop looking at your blog from the perspective of a blogger.

There are various steps that you can take in coming up with the best blog monetization strategy.

In this section, we will take a look at these various steps.

Identifying What the Market Wants

Earlier in this book, we discussed the niche selection process with a focus on building a blog around your interests and passions. Considering this aspect when developing the blog is crucial.

In selecting a niche, you have to go beyond identifying your passion. It is vital that you also look at the type of market you are getting into. What this entails is you looking at the various niches in an industry you have an interest in.

What is the audience in the various niches searching for? What outcomes do they desire? How large is the market?

A blog that will earn a lot of money must be able to offer its readers a specific outcome. If you don't understand this vividly, then assume you have an interest in finance. In the finance industry, your blog can fall into the personal finance niche.

This is a niche that has a broad audience always in search of new information to save money, invest, and control their spending. The information they are searching for are the outcomes you can offer.

In your monetization strategy, you can focus on providing tips, online courses, and a spreadsheet that assists your readers in creating and following a budget. From this point, you can go into other areas like the best investment options and how to save money the right way.

The outcome of the blog will be an improvement in the personal finance of the readers. This outcome is the product you are selling, and readers are always searching to buy this product.

Expanding Your Sources of Incoming Traffic

Monetizing your blog will only be effective if there is constant traffic to your blog.

Regardless of the number of loyal audience members you currently have, there is a need to attract new audience members.

You don't expect the same audience members to keep purchasing the same product over and over.

To improve the traffic to your blog, you must be willing to explore other sources. Twitter, YouTube, Instagram, LinkedIn, Facebook, Reddit, and several other social platforms are excellent sources of blog traffic.

The content formats can also vary in the same manner.

Posting videos, images, and podcasts; using paid advertising; and incorporating search engine optimization (SEO) all play a crucial role in generating the right amount of traffic to your blog.

Developing the Hub of the Business

In developing a monetization strategy, you have to pay close attention to your blog. You must transform it from a basic blog where you share opinions to one on which the content of each post is curated with a goal.

The goal of the content is to generate conversions from your blog visitors.

This means offering the best you can to make people see the blog as one with value. The blog becomes an environment for content marketing. It is from this hub that you diversify into other forms of marketing.

There are steps you must take to optimize your blog for lead generation and conversions.

The first is getting them to sign up on your email list through value, lead magnets, and an opt-in form. You will also need chatbots and autoresponders to work on generating these leads.

To simplify this process, the goal of this hub (your blog) at this point is to convert that random strangers on your blog to a blog subscriber.

You must also be willing to engage in other actions like retargeting. This will enable your paid advertising strategies to pay off. If a visitor opens your page once and closes it, they will forget the name of the site in a few hours. Retargeting is a way of reminding them of the name and existence of your blog.

Now you can reach those visitors who didn't subscribe on the first visit. Imagine how many potential customers you will lose without this option. There are various options when you want to implement the retargeting strategy. These include Google and Facebook.

This is how you develop your blog into a business hub. It focuses on capturing every visitor to make it easy to turn them into paying customers.

Leads Acquisition

A monetization strategy must include a way to get your visitors to show interest in what you are selling. Anyone who can indicate this interest in your product is a lead.

So how do you identify a lead? A person who shows interest in your business will perform any of the following actions:

- Place a call to your business
- Interact with your business through live chat, chatbot, and any other chat option
- Enroll for your webinar
- Become an email list subscriber
- Complete a free test or quiz

For a visitor to take any of these actions, it is an indication that they want to get to know you, and it is an opportunity for you to get to know them. It is up to you to make the most of this opportunity. This is the build-up of gaining a potential customer, and you must build a stable relationship.

As mentioned in the chapter discussing email marketing, you need to offer a lead magnet for this purpose. An opt-in form is also essential. Remember to place the forms at a position that it is easy to get the attention of the lead.

Sales Generation

Your strategy must include a sales generation aspect. This is how you make money from the blog. These include the product page on your blog. For most blogs (including yours), this page only becomes relevant after getting a visitor to become a lead.

If you are familiar with the term "sales funnel," that is what this aspect is all about. The design of this funnel must move your leads from top to bottom effectively. This is the point at which they become customers.

Your funnel might include multiple offers of different prices or a single offer for your readers. The cheapest offer, which you can call the front-end offer, is there to get you a customer. It comes at a price that a lead can pay without feeling it much.

The next offer, which is your core offer, can be a consultation service, training course, or membership site.

The final offer is the high-end offer, which yields the most profit for you. This can be affiliate products, coaching, or follow-up sales.

To effectively move your leads down the sales funnel, you need to implement the use of an autoresponder sequence in addition to your retargeting strategies.

You prepare these emails in advance and have them sent to your leads at a later date.

Growing Your Community

This is the final step in the monetization strategy, and it is an outcome of your long-term thinking. The idea here is simple. What if a lead doesn't buy from you?

There is no need to be bitter about this. The future is always full of surprises. To be prepared for these surprises, you must solidify your relationship with these leads. That is why you need to have a community.

It is through this community that you can continue to provide value to your leads. There are various ways to grow your community. It can be through email newsletters, blog content, podcasts, social media updates, videos, live chat, and many more.

Consistency is vital, and it will surely pay off later.

How Much Can You Make Blogging?

The amount you make blogging is dependent on your effort. Placing a figure on this amount will be impossible. Different blogs attract different individuals.

Despite these facts, you can surely get a range when determining your possible income from blogging. To give you this range, there is a look at how much several popular bloggers make every month.

This gives you an insight into how much you can make from blogging.

On the list (Dizon, 2019), the top-paid blogger earns as much as $125,000 per month. On the same list, the lowest-earning blogger makes at least $1,500 per month. These figures are just an estimate and should only serve as a guide.

Conclusion

The purpose of this book was to give you an in-depth look at how to make money through blogging. The information in this book covered the various aspects of blogging that will be crucial in achieving this goal.

The first chapter was an introduction to blogging. There was a simple definition of what a blog is as well as some features that you can use in identifying a blog on the internet. I also gave you some solid reasons why you should start your blog today in addition to the most crucial being to make money.

In developing a successful blog, the framework of your blog plays a crucial role. This framework consists of the topic of your blog, as well as the niche, name, and goals of the blog. I also gave a few tips that can help drive your blog toward success.

To get on to the goal of monetizing your blog, you need to have a blog. This involves creating one of any of the available platforms like WordPress, Blogger, Tumblr, and so on.

These are popular platforms with unique blogging characteristics.

Although blogging focuses on the use of plain text, consistent changes in the way we blog have resulted in the use of other formats.

Now, you must take advantage of the possibility to include an image or video on your blog and also get yourself used to the idea of podcasting.

These are content formats that a lot of your target audience will be searching for.

Once you have your blog set up with high-quality content, you must look for means to promote your blog. There are numerous options available to do this.

These include networking, guest posting, SEO, repurposing content, and many more. We cannot forget the most important of these promotional tools — social media platforms. Your audience is scattered around the internet, and you have to reach them wherever they are.

The next discussion was a look at how to make money from your blog. A lot of bloggers are already doing it, so why should you be left out? Blogging can be a lucrative venture if you implement the right tactics.

That is what this chapter is all about. It gives you various ideas on how to make money blogging.

There was also a look at how to promote a blog through email marketing. This a separate topic because of how effective it can be in generating income.

Focusing on email marketing as your only promotional tactic to make money on your blog will still yield you a decent amount of steady income.

Understanding how to implement email marketing will have a significant impact on your revenue stream. There is also a need to create a monetization strategy for a steady flow of revenue.

Understanding how to develop one such strategy was my final gift to you. Don't overlook how valuable it is to your goals.

Blogging remains a very profitable venture that offers you the opportunity to take charge of your life both in your finances and the way you use your time. Nonetheless, there is one thing I want you to take away from everything in this book. It is the fact that a successful blog takes time.

Be patient as you build your blog and keep trying out the various tips to find what works best for you as an individual.

References

Andre, M. (2019). The definitive guide to choosing a blog monetization strategy. Retrieved from https://profitblitz.com/blog-monetization-strategy/

Biddulph, R. (2019). 10 smart ways to promote your blog on social media. Retrieved from https://www.shoutmeloud.com/promote-blog-social-media.html

Dizon, A. (2019). How much do bloggers make in 2019?. Retrieved from https://fitsmallbusiness.com/how-much-do-bloggers-make/

Duermyer, R. (2019). Top tips to making money on your blog or website using Google AdSense. Retrieved from https://www.thebalancesmb.com/making-money-from-your-website-with-google-adsense-1794557

Ellering, N. (2019). How to promote your blog with 107 content promotion tactics. Retrieved from https://coschedule.com/blog/how-to-promote-your-blog/#socialmedia

Fernandez, M. (2019). 69 super effective lead magnet ideas to grow your email list in 2019. Retrieved from https://optinmonster.com/9-lead-magnets-to-increase-subscribers/

Goins, J. (2019). 3 ways guest posting can help grow your online audience. Retrieved from https://goinswriter.com/guest-posting/

Newcomer, C. (2019). How to create a WordPress blog in 15 minutes — free guide for 2019. Retrieved from https://themeisle.com/blog/how-to-create-a-blog/

Patel, N. (2019). Affiliate marketing made simple: A step-by-step guide. Retrieved from https://neilpatel.com/what-is-affiliate-marketing/

Rampton, J. (2019). 25 ways to make money from your blog. Retrieved from https://www.forbes.com/sites/johnrampton/2017/11/09/25-ways-to-make-money-from-your-blog/#196afb634892

Risley, D. (2019). Blog monetization: the exact business model to make money blogging (2019). Retrieved from https://www.blogmarketingacademy.com/blog-monetization-strategy/

Wise, A. (2019). 12 blog monetization strategies used to make $124,074. Retrieved from https://www.jeffbullas.com/12-blog-monetization-strategies-used-make-124074-per-month/

Made in the USA
San Bernardino, CA
25 February 2020